FARMERS ON THE MOVE

FARMERS ON THE MOVE

THE STORY OF HOW KISANS ORGANIZED IN MAHARASHTRA

AJIT NAVALE

TRANSLATED BY MEDHA KALE

INTRODUCTION BY P. SAINATH

AFTERWORD BY ASHOK DHAWALE

LeftWord

First published by LeftWord Books in April 2022
Digital print edition, April 2022

LeftWord Books
2254/2A, Shadi Khampur
New Ranjit Nagar
New Delhi 110008
INDIA

LeftWord Books and Vaam Prakashan are imprints of
Naya Rasta Publishers Pvt. Ltd.

leftword.com

ISBN   978-93-92018-38-1 (Paperback)
          978-93-92018-39-8 (e-book)

Originally published in Marathi as
Shetkaryanchi Fauz Nighe:
Goshta Shetkari Sampachi
Aitihasik Long Marchchi
by Samakaleen Prakashan, Pune, 2019

Visit website

To my farmer parents!
At a loss for words.
What do I say?
I owe everything to them.
Everything.

Contents

Introduction

P. Sainath

'We are here with the idea we can file PILs against the overnment of Maharashtra,' they said. 'But we need to understand the issues, to figure out what should be the grounds on which we file.'

The agitated young lawyers were buttonholing me in Azad Maidan in Mumbai, insisting I answer their questions at once. They were impatient to get on with it. In the background, members of the bank employees' unions were moving amongst the crowd trying to distribute water packets. With them were many teachers and students from local colleges.

Were those doctors from J.J. Hospital I was seeing treating poor Adivasis whose feet were bleeding? They were, and there were other doctors too. Nobody had summoned or mobilized them. They just showed up at Azad Maidan in Mumbai, inspired by the moving scenes they had seen on television news.

And bemused media persons, a few of whom had never seen an Adivasi farmer up close (a couple of young ones needed me to confirm that that was who they were looking at: which tribe? – they wanted to know) demanded I address incredibly complex issues in crisp soundbites.

No, mercifully, the media were not focusing on me. Their difficulty was that they knew little or nothing of the lives and livelihoods, dreams and demands of those on whom they now had to focus: 40,000 farmers, overwhelmingly Adivasis, who had marched 182 kilometres from Nashik to Mumbai, across hill and dale, in temperatures over 38°C and inching towards 40°C. Mostly barefoot, some with bleeding feet, in what will forever be remembered as the *Long March to Mumbai*. These farmers had converged on the megapolis under the banner of the All-India Kisan Sabha (AIKS) to berate their government for its many betrayals of their demands. Those were multiple: correct implementation of the Forest Rights Act, recognising the ownership of the tribals over the land they had lived on for generations – from which they were now to be evicted as 'encroachers', pensions for farmers, the main recommendations of the M.S. Swaminathan-led National Farmers' Commission (including the Minimum Support Price formula it called for), proper implementation of the state-announced loan waiver, and more.

So there I was, suddenly pitchforked into the role of interlocutor – since the media vaguely recognizes me as someone connected to the 'rural' and as this guy who can't stop talking about the 'agrarian crisis' – whatever that means.

My own attention was fixed on the marchers. Having tramped six days and nights in awful conditions with astonishing discipline, they were within the perimeter of Mumbai on the night of 11 March. The idea was they would rest and set out early in the morning and reach Azad Maidan by noon or so of the 12 March. Instead, they decided to march the same night and get there much earlier despite being stressed and exhausted. And so they marched, 40,000 silent people, no slogans, surely the most spectacular march of its kind in Mumbai.

The reason? They had learned that lakhs of children would sit for their board exams the next day, 12 March. 'We didn't want to disrupt the traffic and thereby the children's exams,' several of them told me. 'And we didn't want to disturb their sleep either.' Hence the silent march. 'Our children, too, write exams, you know?' said one of the women farmers.

12 March 2018 was a day to remember.

I will, forever.

Yet, it was one culmination of a process that had seen other spectacular action. Earlier, the 11-day Maharashtra farmers' strike of June 2017 was perhaps the first and most effective strike of its kind in the history of the peasant movement here. Every effort at the betrayal of that battle – and there were several – was confronted head-on and beaten back by the same body under whose banner the Nashik-Mumbai marchers streamed into Azad Maidan on 12 March 2018 – the AIKS.

The strike was statewide. Its impact was nationwide. So was that of the Nashik march. The strike brought the report of the National Commission for Farmers back into the limelight years after it had been buried by state and central governments. In the following year, wherever I went in the country, I found farmers everywhere I visited knew of the report, and they wanted its recommendations implemented. In the way-out villages of Punjab, Tamil Nadu, Odisha, Rajasthan, farmers knew the words: Swaminathan Commission. Everywhere, too, they had heard of the Nashik-Mumbai march and demanded to be told more about it.

Want to understand those struggles in Maharashtra? Want to know how they unfolded? How was an insensitive state government – focused on doling out bonanzas for builders – compelled to announce the partial loan waiver for farmers – how did Maharashtra's farmers regain their confidence?

Read this book. Its author was one of the leading participants in those tumultuous events.

WHAT IS AN 'AGRARIAN CRISIS'?

It is hard to overstate the extent of policy-driven devastation inflicted on farmers in this country. As also to exaggerate the extent to which Maharashtra's farmers were the worst affected. It's worth remembering that neo-liberal economics, including liberalization and privatization, began operating here in this state a few years before its deployment in the rest of the country in 1991. With the fire-sale of public assets and resources to the private sector, the closure of the textile mills (those localities now turned into some of the costliest real estate in the world). The at-first-surreptitious and later open acquiring of farmland for the corporate sector. It all happened here first. Under the previous Congress governments – followed by a sharp acceleration of all these policies under the BJP government that succeeded them.

What is this 'agrarian crisis' we speak of? In some Indian languages, we translate this as *krishi sankat*. I use that term, too, but only in a limited way. And I confess I'm dissatisfied with it. The agrarian crisis is larger than just one of farming. The crisis is a very wide one, but the media's grasp of it is very narrow – and is limited to agriculture. Particularly, the 'national media' where many great commentators (not reporters) use the words 'rural', 'agriculture', and 'agrarian' interchangeably. They are, however, very far from being the same thing.

When we speak of agriculture, we obviously refer to the communities linked directly to cultivation, such as farmers and agricultural labourers. 'Agrarian' is something much larger, including all those communities that may not be in any way connect to direct cultivation but whose lives are pretty much dependent on how agriculture is doing. That would include weavers, carpenters, inland fisherfolk, forestry workers, and perhaps scores of other occupational groups.

Any crisis in farming rocks the lives and livelihoods of these occupational groups. In Anantapur, Andhra Pradesh, for instance, or in Pochampally (now in Telangana), the suicides of weavers in the early and mid-1990s often preceded the suicides of farmers. Why? Because when farmers went bankrupt, the weavers lost their first market. Likewise, when farming went bust, the village carpenter starved. The average *mistry* (carpenter) family in a village would receive about a third of its payment for their services in cash. The rest – the farmers paid them in produce – so many kilos of rice, so many kilos of vegetables, and so on.

Farmers and farming are thus central to the well-being of not just their own families but of all these millions of other livelihoods as well. If farmers do poorly, it affects not just agriculture but also the entire agrarian and even the larger rural economy. Rural, of course, refers to a larger entity than both agriculture and agrarian – with 833 million human beings living in rural India according to the 2011 Census. You have many miners, construction or even industrial workers living in what we understand to be rural areas. All of them are badly affected when farming is devastated – the first area of impact obviously being food.

The wealthy state of Maharashtra is also notorious for malnourishment (or even starvation deaths) amongst hungry people, mainly Adivasi children. In September 2016, the Bombay High Court had pulled up the BJP-Fadanavis government over such deaths. It was revealed in the court proceedings that 17,000 persons, including women and children, had died due to malnutrition in the state in the preceding year. Many of the deceased were themselves farm labourers or marginal farmers unable to make ends meet. That had plenty to do with the larger agrarian crisis.

Therefore, to say farmers and farming are central to our nation's well-being is no exaggeration.

It's also important to know that there is no definition of 'rural' in the Indian Census. There is a definition of 'urban unit' or town. That refers to places that have a municipality, corporation, cantonment board, notified town area committee etc., That definition would also apply to other places (Census towns) which have a minimum population of 5,000, a density of population of at least 400 per square kilometre, and where at least 75 per cent of the male workforce are engaged in non-agricultural pursuits.

As one Census 2011 paper puts it: 'All areas which are not

categorized as Urban areas are considered as Rural Areas'. In short – anything that's not urban is rural.

WHO IS A FARMER? HOW MANY DO WE HAVE IN INDIA?

The Census records two kinds of cultivators: 'main workers' and 'marginal workers'. The latter is more like agricultural labourers or non-farm workers since *farming is not their main activity.* A 'main worker' in cultivation is someone for whom that is the major occupation for *at least half the year.* That group makes up barely 8 per cent of the population as a whole. Yes, full-time farmers as officially defined – if we go by the Census of India – account for *less than 8 per cent of our population, or 95.8 million people,* in the 2011 Census. If we add to that figure those who farm for less than six months – that is, the 22.8 million 'marginal cultivators' – then too, it would come to under 10 per cent of our population.

Between 1981 and 1991, the number of 'main cultivators' actually went up from 92 million to over 110 million. But after that – the decline is steep. Between the 1991 Census (over 110 million farmers) and the 2011 Census, the population of 'main cultivators' fell *by nearly 15 million.* That means, on average, that's about 2,035 farmers losing 'main cultivator' status every single day for the last 20 years. And in a time of jobless growth, they've had few places to go beyond the lowest, menial ends of the service sector. In Bengaluru, you will find once proud farmers from Mandya district joining the IT sector – yes, to serve as cooks and waiters in the canteens of some big companies.

Even if you count together all cultivators and agricultural labourers, the number would be around 263 million or 22 per cent of the population. It is imperative to know these facts if we are to at all understand the farmer suicide numbers. Why? After all, every suicide should be a matter of concern. But that is not how so many of our 'experts' see it. They view it purely in terms of what percentage of farmers have killed themselves. If the total population of farmers is 100 and 10 take their own lives – that is 10 per cent – a very high figure. But if the total number was 1,000 and 10 take their own lives, that's only 1 per cent. And for the 'experts' – that is negligible.

So, if half of the population of India are farmers – that would be 600-650 million people. Since suicide victims since 1995 number 310,000 farmers, that would be 0.05 per cent of the population of farmers. And for the experts, this means it is unimportant as a statistic. That over three lakh farmers have taken their own lives becomes a mathematical issue, not a moral one. Yet, it is also bad math, as we shall see.

If the 310,000 figure is calculated as a percentage of 95.8 million (the Census count of farmers), then the figure you get is six and a half times higher than the 0.05 per cent the experts want to believe. Yet, even this is a minimal way of understanding the suicide numbers and extremely misleading if we do not in 2008 factor in other numbers and ratios, as well. Now, one gentleman from Maharashtra persisted with the percentages approach and ended up proudly finding that his state was not the worst in India for farmers' suicides but only the fourth worst. This he did at the behest of the then Vilasrao Deshmukh government.

He delivered what the government wanted. And did me the honour of naming me on the front page of the Mumbai Mirror as an enemy of the state. (To this day, coming from him, I wear that abuse like a badge of honour). He was duly rewarded by both state and central governments.

So, which did he find were the worst states and why? Puducherry and Goa – by his methods – would be the worst states for farmer suicides! Yes, you would get terrible percentages because these states have hardly any farmers.

Let me explain: if there are three farmers in Malabar Hill, Mumbai, and one of these three kills himself – that would, in this twisted logic, make Malabar Hill the worst place on Planet earth for farmers' suicides. After all, one-third of its farmer population have become suicide victims. Of course, you'd have to be completely clueless to understand that it that way, wouldn't you?

In the year of the Census 2011, Goa recorded one farmer suicide and Puducherry none. The same year, Maharashtra saw 3,337. Between 1995 and 2015 – *Maharashtra logged close to 65,000 farmer suicides.* In other words, every fifth farmer in India taking their own life is from this state.

Yet, far more distinguished 'experts' than the discoverer of farm suicides in Puducherry have lined up to discredit themselves. It's fascinating how this country's much-acclaimed experts, including celebrated economists like Jagdish Bhagwati and Arvind Panagariya, share and amplify this ignorance.

These two gentlemen, both Professors at Columbia University, USA, wrote in their book *India's Tryst With Destiny*: 'at least half of the Indian workforce is engaged in farming. This fact points to a much lower suicide rate per 100,000 individuals for farmers than in the general population'. Note how easily those *'engaged in farming'* become *'farmers!'*

How I wish someone would explain to these experts that everyone dependent on agriculture is not a farmer. In the same way that everybody working in Bollywood is not an actor, much less a hero. Or in the same way, everybody working in the education sector is not a student or a teacher. There are millions of others involved in those sectors too.

Bhagwati and Panagariya, in fact, go on to mock farmers' suicides – indeed to ridicule it as a trivial issue.

Their understanding goes something like this: After all, 53 out of every 100 Indians are farmers. So our 270,940 farm suicides since 1995 are a low number on a population base of over 600 million. So low that we should be agitated over *how the suicide rate in the general population can be brought 'down to the levels prevailing amongst farmers'.*

Never mind, for now, the appalling moral position that a quarter of a million human beings are taking their lives (which figure has crossed 3.1 lakh since their book came out) is hardly alarming. The Bhopal gas tragedy, the worst industrial disaster in human terms, claimed over 20,000 lives. But in this perverse logic, since that was less than 0.003 per cent of the then population, it is rendered meaningless. That position says more about its authors than about the suicides. It speaks as much about their ethics as about their academics. It shows they are clueless about who a farmer is. Also, they know nothing of what an Indian farmer's life is like.

And yet, we need more factors to be looked at besides the above. Sure, absolute numbers and percentages are important. But we also need to consider, for example, farmers' suicides as a share of all suicides in the state – farmers' suicides as a share of all suicides in the country – *and* the suicide rate of farmers per 100,000 cultivators. Prof. K. Nagaraj, then of the Madras Institute of Development Studies and one of India's most brilliant economists, brought all these measures together and found that Maharashtra had 'become the graveyard of farmers'.

Although Maharashtra has seen more than 65,000 farmer suicides, we cannot even know approximate numbers. Why? Because the government at the Centre found the suicide numbers an embarrassment. From 2014, it began to distort the methodology of the National Crime Records Bureau, an important unit of the Union Home Ministry and the one authoritative source collating suicide numbers in India. As a result, farm suicide data from 2015 became incomparable with the preceding 19 years of data on the same subject. Yet, the suicide figures kept mounting.

In August 2017, the Modi government got so fed up with rising criticism on the suicides issue – it simply shut down the NCRB and merged it into a little-known body called the Bureau of Police Research & Development (BPRD). Having done so, it found it had hurt itself badly as the NCRB also provided other vital data that the BPRD had no capability to do. Ten months later, by April 2018, it de-merged the NCRB from the BPRD and re-constructed it from the ashes! However, the BJP government has not allowed the NCRB to publish suicide data from 2016 onwards. So we simply do not know how many more farmers have taken their own lives since then.

Since 2000, it has been my misfortune as a national-level reporter on the suicide issue to visit around 900 households spread across seven states where a farmer had taken their life. Many of those households were in this state, primarily in Vidarbha and Marathwada. That experience scarred me and those of dear friends and fellow journalists like Jaideep Hardikar for life. I keep thinking: it shattered my mind and health and disturbed me forever. If that is what did it to me, what must it have done to the farmers of Maharashtra? Never forget, for every farmer who took their life, tens of thousands did not but were in the same state of despair.

Add to this that several regions of the state have been in the grip for a while of serious Climate Change – a subject that barely exists in public discourse in India. For all the devastation it has caused our farmers – have you seen a single day's – or a single hour's discussion – of that subject in either parliament or the Maharashtra Legislature? Here we are, a state that had several years of drought in the last ten years. Parts of which are presently reeling under unprecedented floods. These come as deadly blows to farmers already crushed by debt, crop failure, or when they have fine harvests – crippling price-drops.

That is why the fightback of farmers in this state is so inspiring, so important – so energising. And very few people are as qualified as Ajit Navale to write this book on their great struggles of these past three years. They have fought back from a state of acute demoralization and are still determinedly in that battle. Abused by so many great experts, abandoned by so many intellectuals we once held in respect, they have not caved in. That is why the agitations led by Navale and his Kisan Sabha colleagues are so vital. They have not just fought the government – they have battled apathy and even thwarted attempted sabotage and betrayals – never losing their dignity or focus. Their achievement has to be seen in the light of the sheer demoralization that had prevailed amongst farmers in Maharashtra.

Those were the thoughts in my mind as I watched 40,000 farmers, overwhelmingly Adivasis from Nashik, among India's poorest citizens, troop into Mumbai's Azad Maidan on 12 March 2018. I felt happy, yet humbled, thrilled yet thoughtful, energized but anxious. That was the day those courageous kisans – whom Poonam Mahajan of the BJP Mumbai dismissed as people misguided by 'urban Maoists' – reminded me of something else – that this was also the state of great revolts by Adivasis, farmers, workers, and other marginal sections. Of the astonishing Warli uprising and the legendary Godavari Parulekar. Of the *prati sarkar* (parallel government) of Satara whose efforts at a provisional underground government went further than any similar attempts in the north under British rule in the twentieth century. The *prati sarkar*, whose leader, Nana Patil, was one of the early presidents of the All-India Kisan Sabha (AIKS) soon after independence. I – trained as a historian – was given an invaluable refresher course in history that morning by the barefoot marchers from Nashik.

THE POLICY POGROMS OF THE NEO-LIBERAL STATE

In Vidarbha, at the turn of the millennium, even as late as 2002, the costs of cultivation were still ensconced in another era. (Unless you had switched to Bt cotton, which had entered illegally by that time). An unirrigated acre of cotton costs around Rs. 4,000 or so to cultivate. If that were an irrigated acre, the cost would be between Rs. 10,000-12,000. (That was when farmers were still using the standard hybrid seeds in the market, while a few used local seeds). Today that would be Rs.20,000 and above for the unirrigated acre and around Rs. 40,000 (in some cases higher) for the irrigated acre. In Maharashtra, liberalization, privatization, and globalization had taken root more firmly than the Bt cotton that farmers were now using. And India was a paid-up member of the World Trade Organization (WTO).

In 15 years, the costs of cultivation had gone up five-fold. But the income of the farmer did not go up five-fold. It stagnated. Corporate profits – those of the companies controlling seeds, fertilizers and pesticides – soared – as did those of the local input dealers who were emerging a new point of capital accumulation in the countryside. Nowhere did the prices received by farmers for their cotton see an increase that was in proportion to the rise in the prices consumers paid for clothing apparel made from that cotton.

None of this was accidental. In session after session of parliament, budget after budget, policies were devised and rammed through – on bank credit, on priority sector lending – one anti-farmer move after another. Agricultural universities, once viewed by farmers as the property of their community, which brought cheap varieties to market for close to two decades, no longer did so. They were pressed into service of and control by the corporate world. Today, there are agricultural universities whose syndicate or other leadership bodies are dominated by input dealers, traders – and very few farmers.

The most tremendous damage came in the area of credit. The corporate media have painted an image of farmers as these shameless, greedy people constantly asking for loan waivers. But never ask themselves why farmers started demanding this – or when. No major kisan organization was raising such a demand in a big way before the year 2000. The last 'waiver' had been when the then Union Agriculture Minister Chaudhury Devi Lal had written off a flat Rs. 10,000 for farmers, cultivators, artisans and weavers by state-run banks in 1990. That, too, had followed some years of great drought.

The demand for a waiver in the past 20 years – no one was asking for one in 1998-99 – came as a massive shift occurred in which agricultural credit went increasingly to non-farmers.

Look at how the National Bank for Agriculture and Rural Development (NABARD) has treated farmers. The State Focus Report of NABARD for 2016-17 allocated 51.3 per cent of nearly Rs. 3 lakh crores of its Potential-linked credit plan (PLP) to Mumbai city and its suburbs. This was 'agricultural credit'!

As *The Hindu*'s Alok Deshpande, who broke that story, reported: 'The disparity in projected loan shares goes beyond Mumbai. As per the report, after excluding the funds projected for Mumbai, estimates of PLPs for Marathwada and Vidarbha are just 16.48 per cent and 16 per cent respectively.'

Where are the farmers in Mumbai? There are very few agriculturists in Mumbai and its suburbs – but there is *a huge concentration of agri-business in Mumbai*. NABARD's allocation was just a reflection of a process already well underway. Studies showed that more than 50 per cent of agricultural credit disbursed through banks was through urban and metro branches in 3 or 4 cities over several years. Less than 40 per cent of such credit was disbursed through rural bank branches. There was also the time when the banks behaved like *sahucars* (moneylenders) themselves when dealing with poor people. In October 2010, The 'Aurangabad group', a band of that city's elite industrialists, executives, doctors, lawyers and other professionals, bought 150 Mercedes Benz cars on a single day. One of those buyers went on to become an MLA from Aurangabad East. By special dispensation of the then chairman of the State Bank of India, no less, the SBI Aurangabad gave them a loan covering almost two-thirds of the Rs. 65 crores deal – at an interest rate of just 7 per cent, yes, 7 per cent!

In that same period, Hirabai Fakira Rathod, an Adivasi woman farmer also in Aurangabad district, paid 15.9 per cent interest to the same public sector banking system for a loan to purchase a tractor. That, of course, bankrupted her in the next few years. Meanwhile, several of the buyers of the Mercedes Benz cars immediately resold those luxury vehicles which they had got on such cheap terms (with the company also throwing in heavy discounts) at high profits! The interest of 15.9 per cent for a tractor and 7 per cent for a loan to buy a Mercedes Benz.

I met the bankrupt Adivasi farmer in 2016 when she had 'slaved to pay back nearly Rs. 9 lakhs' as she put it, on an original loan of Rs. 5.75 lakhs. The bank closed the loan there as a 'one-time settlement' – as if it were doing her a great favour.

We starved the farmer of credit by policy fiat. And we did this at the very moment we were encouraging corporations to resort to price-gouging on inputs – in the name of 'market-based pricing.'

Where a *750-gram packet* of hybrid seeds used to cost Rs.300 to 350 till 2002, Bt cotton seed started selling around at Rs. 1,650 to Rs. 1,800 for a *packet of 450 grams.* This continued until legal action initiated by the then Andhra Pradesh government in 2004 brought down the Bt price to Rs. 925. But millions of farmers had been fleeced by that time. Likewise, a 50-kilo bag of Di-ammonia phosphate was less than Rs. 200 a kilogram in 1991 today costs around Rs. 1,400.

Newer and newer methods of literally cheating the farmer were devised by governments acting as *dalals* (brokers) of seed companies.

Agriculture was de-regulated to an extent where the quality of seed has for 15 years now been officially graded much lower. Before the 'reforms' period, when you bought a seed bag, you would see the minimum germination rate (MGR) stamped on its reverse. It used to be 85 per cent or so. That meant a minimum of 85 per cent of the bag's contents would work, i.e., germinate. In Andhra Pradesh, in 2004, farmers pointed out to me that the MGR had been reduced quietly to 60 per cent. Governments were entering into MOUs with seed companies that allowed them to lower standards.

What does MGR being down to 60 per cent mean? It means that if a village buys 10,000 bags of seed, they are paying for 10,000 bags (and much higher prices than before 1991) – *but they are getting 6,000 bags* – really speaking.

Across India, the cost of every single input soared and, with it, the misery of the farmer.

Every five years, as the elections approached, central and state governments would make huge promises to the farmer – particularly in Maharashtra. Remember Vilasrao Deshmukh's promise of a procurement price increase of Rs. 500 per quintal – before the 2004 assembly elections?

What did his government do after coming to power? They had made a promise of Rs. 2,700 a quintal, but in reality *lowered the procurement price by Rs. 500 by withdrawing* the so-called 'advance bonus' payment.

With that, the government of Maharashtra removed Rs. 1,200 crores from the farmers. What it did next was crazy. The Chief Minister announced a 'package' of Rs. 1,075 crores to help the distressed farmers. A package of Rs. 1,075 crore was being given to people from whom he had taken away Rs. 1,200 crore!

US-EU SUBSIDIES DESTROY COTTON PRICES

At the same time, the USA and the European Union were drowning their cotton growers in subsidies. Cotton growers of the USA are not small farmers; they are companies – corporations. In Maharashtra, cotton growers number in millions. How many 'cotton growers' were there in the USA at the time? Barely 20,000!

On a total crop value of 3.9 billion dollars in 2005, the United States gave its cotton growers a subsidy of 4.7 billion dollars! It had also pumped in subsidies with devastating results in the late 1990s. Cotton prices which had ruled at 90 to 100 cents a pound in 1994-95, fell to around 40 cents a pound, and from late 1998, suicides began all over the world as prices crashed and farmers ran up horrible losses.

In Burkina Faso, scores of cotton farmers killed themselves. In July 2003, the Presidents of Burkina Faso and Mali wrote a letter published in the *New York Times*, 'Your Farm Subsidies are Strangling Us'. But India failed to take action against such subsidies then. Our duties on cotton at the time were 5 per cent. And if you were a Mumbai textile magnate, then you did not pay even that 5 per cent. You got it waived in lieu of export of garments.

Each new policy under neo-liberal regimes hastened the collapse of restraint on corporate power. The Indian state had downgraded the farmer and withdrawn its protection to them. Further measures were pushed, which made access to credit even more difficult for the farmer.

The results were predictable. Millions of farmers across the country were forced to go back to the *sahucars*. Debt exploded.

The June 2019 Financial Stability Report of the RBI shows us that 55 per cent of *all* credit (loans above Rs. 5 crores) from public sector banks goes to corporate houses. And that of this 55 per cent – a staggering 87 per cent has been classified as non-performing assets. Yet, the corporate-owned media propagate the fiction that poor farmers and their loans are responsible for the NPAs burdening the PSU banks!

The BJP has shown that it can not only continue the policies of its predecessor governments ruthlessly but can go much further – more aggressively!

In 2014, the Modi government came to power with an election promise they would immediately implement a Minimum Support Price of Cost of Production plus 50 per cent. That was one of the critical recommendations of the Swaminathan Commission's report.

By 2015, it declared in a court affidavit, and in an RTI reply, this was not feasible and would, in fact – 'distort market prices'.

In 2016, union agriculture minister Radha Mohan Singh denied that the BJP had ever made such a promise.

In 2017, the BJP tom-tommed the superiority of the agriculture 'model' of then Madhya Pradesh chief minister Shivraj Chauhan. That campaign lost its sheen when his government gunned down five protesting farmers in Mandsaur.

In 2018, finance minister Arun Jaitley claimed in his budget speech that the 2014 promise had already been implemented!

Meanwhile, policy after policy that decimated the farmers' security was also presented to the nation as a lifeline for farmers, as a great revival.

The mantra since late 2017 has been around the Pradhan Mantri Fasal Bima Yojana or crop insurance scheme. The corporate world was allowed to take over this sector – with public sector insurance entities to wet-nurse them. As an RTI in *The Tribune*, Chandigarh showed in November 2018, in the first 24 months of the scheme, 18 corporations (including 13 private ones) made Rs. 15,795 crores in profit. That means raking in profit at an average of over Rs. 21 crores each day for two years.

All this while, the BJP government seems quite happy to present a poor case in the Supreme Court on an issue of hanging fire – the ongoing forest land rights case.

There is no front on which the Indian farmer does not have to struggle for a living today.

But if Maharashtra was the state where the worst things happened to farmers, it is also the state where some of the best responses to their crisis have come from farmers themselves.

And back at Azad Maidan on 12 March 2018: For the first time in my 36 years in Mumbai, I saw the middle classes and other non-farmers turn out in such numbers for the oppressed cultivators. That day, my friends and I saw lawyers who came there for farmers. Doctors for farmers. Teachers for farmers, students for farmers. Techies for farmers. Vendors and business people for farmers. It dawned on me that we witnessed something special: a nation for farmers. In microcosm, yes, but genuinely so.

That was the beginning of the idea of the middle-class forum of Nation for Farmers, which went on to play a role in helping over 100 farmers organizations mobilize for the great march that followed in Delhi in November 2018, one where 21 political parties appeared on the farmers' platform to pledge support to the demands of the farmers.

The agrarian crisis has long since gone beyond the agrarian. It's a crisis of society. Maybe even a civilizational crisis, with perhaps the largest body of small farmers and labourers on earth fighting to save their livelihoods. The agrarian crisis is no longer just a measure of loss of land, nor only a measure of loss of human life, jobs or productivity. It is a measure of our own loss of humanity, of the shrinking boundaries of our humaneness. For the past twenty years, we have sat by and watched the deepening misery of the dispossessed, including the death by suicide of well over 300,000 farmers. While some – including famous economists and intellectuals – have mocked the enormous suffering around us and even denied the existence of a crisis.

The struggle is very far from over. But here are some of the things we learned and put together at the Nation for Farmers, lessons drawn from the lives and experiences of everyday farmers and farm labourers.

We need to keep alive the central recommendations of the Swaminathan Commission. It is astonishing how farmers in remote regions, disconnected from organized politics, have heard of this (National) Commission for Farmers and how badly they want it respected and implemented.

The Commission, which created, probably, the first-ever blueprint for Indian agriculture, held extraordinarily wide consultations across the country, with farmers, labourers, farm organizations, and many others, submitted its first report in December 2004 and the fifth in October 2006. For fifteen years, those reports have languished without a single hour of dedicated discussion in parliament. They deserve to be discussed, updated and honoured in not just parliament but in the legislature of every state and union territory.

Here's what we suggest:

That parliament hold a three-week special session dedicated entirely to the crisis and related issues. A joint session of both houses. When it came to passing the GST bill for the corporate sector, parliament could be summoned at extremely short notice, the President himself came down for a joint special session of both houses, and the whole matter concluded in no time.

Surely, the hundreds of millions who constitute the agrarian population deserve as much importance as the corporate sector? And they have waited for fifteen years.

HOLD THAT SPECIAL SESSION OF PARLIAMENT

On what principles would that session be based? The Indian Constitution. Specifically, that crucially important part of it – the Directive Principles of State Policy. That chapter speaks of a need to 'minimize the inequalities in income' and 'endeavour to eliminate inequalities in status, facilities, opportunities . . .' . The principles call for 'a social order in which justice, social, economic and political, shall inform all the institutions of the national life'.

The right to work, to education, to social security. The raising of the level of nutrition and public health. The right to a better standard of living. Equal pay for equal work for men and women. Just and humane conditions of work. These are amongst the main principles. The Supreme Court has more than once said the Directive Principles are as important as our Fundamental Rights. If the Fundamental Rights are the heart of the Constitution, the Directive Principles are its soul.

An agenda for the special session? Some suggestions that others concerned by the situation can amend or add to:

Three days for discussion of the Swaminathan Commission report. Almost fifteen years overdue! It submitted five reports between December 2004 and October 2006 that cover a multitude of vital issues and not just Minimum Support Price. Those include productivity, profitability, sustainability, technology and technology fatigue, dryland farming, price shocks and stabilization, and much more. We also need to halt the privatization of agricultural research and technology. And deal with impending ecological disasters.

Three days for people's testimony. Let victims of the crisis speak from the floor of parliament's central hall and tell the nation what the crisis is about, what it has done to them and countless millions of others. And it's not just about farming. But the devastation that surging privatization of health and education has done the rural poor, indeed all the poor. Health expenditures are the fastest or second-fastest-growing component of rural family debt.

Three days for credit crisis. The unrelenting rise of indebtedness. This has been a huge driving factor in the suicide deaths of countless thousands of farmers, apart from devastating millions of others. Often it has meant the loss of much or all of their land. Policies on institutional credit paved the way for the return of the moneylender.

Three days for the country's mega water crisis. It's much greater than a drought. This government seems determined to push through the privatization of water in the name of 'rational pricing'. We need the right to drinking water established as a fundamental human right – and the banning of privatization of this life-giving resource in any sector. Ensuring social control and equal access, particularly to the landless.

Three days for the rights of women farmers. The agrarian crisis cannot be resolved without engaging with the rights – including those of ownership – and problems of those who do the most work in the fields and farms. While in the Rajya Sabha, Prof. Swaminathan introduced The Women Farmers' Entitlements Bill, 2011 (lapsed in 2013) that could still provide a starting point for this debate.

Three days for the issues of landless labourers, both women and men. With mounting distress migrations in many directions, this crisis is no longer just rural. Where it is, any public investment made in agriculture has to factor in their needs, rights, and perspective.

Three days debate on agriculture: What kind of farming do we want twenty years from now? One driven by corporate profit? Or by communities and families for whom it is the basis of their existence? We need to press for other forms of ownership and control in agriculture, like the vigorous *Sangha Krishi* (group farming) efforts of Kerala's Kudumbashree movement. And we need to revive the unfinished agenda of land reform.

You could say the battles for this unfinished agenda began anew in Maharashtra in June 2017. The author of this book, Dr Ajit Navale, was at the forefront of those struggles and gives us a coherent yet passionate account and analysis of the farmers' strike, its features, and its fallout. Navale was the Convenor of the Coordination Committee of Farmers Organizations that led the strike. He was an organizer and leader in the historic Nashik-Mumbai march. This is a book by a participant in the making of history, for our times, and for future generations. Don't fail to read it.

The farmers of Maharashtra have reached out to the rest of us. Can we rise to the occasion and their expectations?

Farmers on the Move

Preface

I am overwhelmed as I narrate this story of a historical strike and the Long March by farmers. I feel so because my heart and soul lies in farming and the soil.

For me, *sheti* (farming) is a beautiful word, just like the word *aai* (mother). I felt secure in the soft soil of our farm, just as I would in my mother's lap. I belonged there; I grew there. Everything about farming is wonderful. Ploughing, sowing, de-weeding, transplanting, harvesting, milling . . . these processes enrich our life, making it beautiful. They give, to each, without bounds. I lived these life-giving processes and celebrated the agri'culture'. My bond with farming and the soil grew closer and closer.

Later in life, I got educated and became independent. I started my own hospital. However, that did not pull me away from farming. It pulled me closer; I breathed it. But I was also the one among many who had to leave farming and go away.

As a child, I remember seeing our lush green fields and piles of grain after the harvest. What I did not see was the economics of it. I did not get it either. And I think it was better that way. But now, those lush green fields and the piles of grain do not fail to remind me of all the loss that farmers are burdened with.

The wealth of the cities and the riches of the few cannot hide the total loss of hope and misery in the countryside. The farmers are helpless. We see how they pine for better days, lose hope, and then choose to end their lives.

I choke. Just like other farmers, I do.

Today, a farmer reels under the impact of all the injustice done to farming and farmers over many generations. She is fighting this injustice on her own. But now, the youngsters from the farming communities have joined this battle to support their parents. They are jostling the existing system. The story of the Farmers' strike and of the Long March is their story, of how they dared the system and showed their might.

The years leading to the agitations were backbreaking for the farmers. Flawed government policies had resulted in the decline of farm prices. Expenses on inputs such as seeds, fertilizers, farm tools, transport, electricity, pesticides, and chemicals had shot up. The farmers could not even recover the cost of inputs, let alone earn a profit. The burden of debt kept increasing. On top of that, natural disasters have made lives even more miserable. A three-year-long severe drought had decimated farmers.

Shattered and desperate, farmers chose death over life. Suicides peaked. In the last fifteen years, Maharashtra witnessed around 20,773 farmer suicides. Children were burying and cremating their farmer parents and siblings all over the state. The government was cruelly silent, turning its back on their plight. The system did nothing to stop this while public speeches, sloganeering and lethargy continued.

On this backdrop of neglect, anger and unrest, these young farmers announced the strike – a strike unlike any India had witnessed before. Later, forty thousand farmers walked from Nashik to Mumbai, covering a distance of 180 kilometres to voice their demands. Both these protests left an indelible mark on the history of the agrarian movement. I was witness to these protests and their thrilling moments.

Farmers' strike and the Long March compelled the state government to agree to their demands. It had to allocate Rs. 34,000 crores for loan waivers, of which Rs. 21,000 crores were transferred to the banks with immediate effect. The state had to take a stand on Minimum Support Price (MSP), equalling the cost of production plus 50 per cent. It also had to transfer ownership titles to the tillers of the land. But for me, the biggest takeaway was the hope instilled in farmers' minds. It looked like the agrarian movement had found its path. The young farmers realized the power of being united and learnt some crucial lessons for future courses of action. Many agrarian issues were discussed during this period. Conflicting positions led to rigorous debates. On the one hand, the demand for loan waivers and MSP was criticized as begging. Some questioned the authority of the state to determine the value of their produce. They wanted no state interference and complete freedom of trade and technology. Loan waivers and subsidies were termed as doles, and any state intervention was outright rejected. For many, the state could not offer any solution because the state itself was a problem.

And others maintained that considering the peculiar position of farming in India, the state and society have to support farmers. For them, loan waivers and MSP was nothing but ways of returning the loot over the years. This position also claimed that the state has to intervene to formulate a comprehensive, dynamic and time-bound policy for sustainable agriculture, in light of the recommendations by the Swaminathan Commission. It also needs to work on areas such as agriculture research, crop insurance, credit, drought eradication, equitable irrigation, farmer-friendly import-export policy, a fair and just share for the farming family in processing and marketing of produce, building basic infrastructure in rural areas, including that for agriculture. The state has to make essential budgetary provisions and cut down production costs. So, the state has to be there.

I felt a strong need to document these debates and dialogue between two differing positions in the farmers' movement.

Some farm leaders blamed cities and urban citizens for the agrarian downfall. They were trying to create a mythical fight between farmers and urban citizens. And then, the Farmers' strike and the Long March told a very different story. One can never forget the solidarity and love shown by the urban people at some critical junctures in both the protests. It was as if the entire humanity was out there to support the farmers. It was necessary to document these experiences so that the future direction of these struggles was well informed.

Some thinkers also argued that demand for MSP was against the interests of the poor. The conflict between farmers and agricultural labourers was another contentious issue. And so was the distribution of water and regional representation. The debates also centred on the ethicality of loan waivers the role of taxpayers and their money. We needed to record these debates, present an alternative policy, and give a new direction to the agrarian issues.

The strike saw many stalwarts in the farmers' movement come together on a common platform. Though it gave a big fillip to the farmers, that unity was short-lived. The need to set aside personal interests for a larger cause was felt more than ever. I believe recording these processes will be a good lesson for the future.

This and other such reasons pushed me to write this book. Many people have helped me document this story. I thank Dr Ashok Dhawale, J. P. Gavit (MLA), Ajit Abhyankar, Dr Dnyaneshwar Mote, Dr Maharudra Dake, Shantaram Gaje, Heramb Kulkarni and Ramesh Jadhav from Agrowan for their support and encouragement. Suhas Kulkarni and Gauri Kanetkar of Samakaleen Prakashan were proactive and ensured that the book reached its readers. Their colleague Sandip Salunkhe designed it well. Veteran journalist P. Sainath wrote the foreword, which was translated to Marathi by our friend, Uday Narkar. My wife, Dr Archana, went through the drafts numerous times and made important suggestions. I am grateful to all of them.

I am aware that people are curious about what happened after the Long March. The state government did relax some rules regarding the loan waiver, which in turn benefitted millions of farmers, but it went back on its promise of increasing the eligibility cut off date to 30 June 2017, resulting in a similar number of farmers being denied the benefits. The government also failed to help those who repay their loans on time. No concrete steps were taken regarding MSP. Kisan Sabha continued its struggle for these demands even after the march. It led a network of 208 farmers' groups for a united protest in the capital. Like the Long March, these 208 organizations held four massive rallies in Delhi on 29 and 30 November 2018. The farmers' issues were back in mainstream discussions.

These protests definitely brought new energy, hope, and confidence to the farming community. They felt alive. I wish that this newfound energy and hope leads us to a new beginning, brings abundance to the fields and smiles on the faces of my beloved farmers. I wish that this energy brings light to everyone around. This is why I wrote this story.

1

Leaving behind the life-sucking crowds of Mumbai, we were heading towards Nashik. The phone kept ringing. I drove with one hand and answered calls with the other. 'Don't use the phone while driving,' Khandubaba warned me. I couldn't afford to miss a single call. The calls were non-stop, a few from journalist friends but mostly from young farmers from different villages. 'Doctor, come what may do not backtrack. We are there to support you,' they were pleading.

Now I knew what it must be like to save a ship from a turbulent storm and guide it safely to the shore. The coup to break the historical strike by farmers was foiled. We needed to boost people's confidence and assure them that the strike was now in committed and trustworthy hands. The centre of the strike had been Puntambe all this while. But now, we needed to ground it somewhere else. Considering all the possibilities, I was heading towards Nashik. The events of the previous night kept playing on my mind. I kept thinking about all that had happened in the last four months.

I had told Rohidas to reach Nashik in the morning. He was the first person to call when I boycotted the meeting with the Chief Minister and left from there. 'What shall we do?' he asked. 'Shall I come to Mumbai? I can bring some youngsters along,' he offered. But it was futile. We needed to give a strong message that the strike was not over. And this could happen only if we could shut down the Agri Produce Market Committees (APMC). I wanted Rohidas and Nilesh to take that responsibility.

Rohidas Dhumal is a committed activist with a keen interest in farming and farmers' issues. He belongs to another political party, but that does not stop him from participating in any activity for the benefit of farmers. I met Nilesh Talekar when he was a member of the Students' Federation of India (SFI). Lately, he had joined many other groups. But as they say, once in the movement, always in the movement. Other spaces come without a sense of belonging. One does not stop thinking about the issues and then returns to the movement. Not everyone can come back. Some pine to return. I thought of many such fellows. They had left the movement, lured by the glamour of the outside world. I quivered and felt sad.

Is it really difficult to be honest with ourselves?

To live the way we feel inside.

I tell you, it is not.

Rohidas and Nilesh had reached Nashik a day before. Traders had got their stocks out, claiming that strike was over. Shops were set up in the APMC premises. The media was reporting from these shops on how the strike was over. Just then, Rohidas and Nilesh reached the APMC. They had called other activists and also some new contacts from social media. They gathered all farmers and traders and narrated the previous night's events. They convinced them to continue the strike. And within minutes, the market, including the shops, was closed. The APMC was shut. The strike was back in the news. It was clear that Nashik was the new centre of the strike. Rohidas and Nilesh had fulfilled their responsibility.

2

It's been two months. The news of farmers' ongoing strike was making rounds. The idea itself was fascinating. The world had witnessed strikes by workers, teachers, students, officers, doctors, and many others. Even the porters and labourers had done that. But did anyone ever imagine that the farmers could go on a strike?

That is why the headlines in newspapers on 2 April 2017

announcing the strike caught everyone's attention. Farmers from Puntambe in Ahmednagar had resolved to do that. They had decided to cultivate only for their own needs and keep the rest of the farm fallow. They had, in fact, passed a resolution to this effect in the gram sabha on 3 April 2017. They had appealed to all the farmers in the state to go on a strike from 1 June. Dhananjay Dhorade had mooted this idea and convinced his young friends. Maharashtra had recently seen a strike by doctors, and another by teachers, right during the annual examinations. The primary and straightforward thought behind the farmers' strike was that if we did not cultivate and work on the farm, the state government would get into trouble, and our demands would be met.

The idea of a strike was interesting. It would have caught people's attention. But, how can a farmer not cultivate his land? How could that be?

Something was prodding me from inside.

Sowing the seed is such a celebration for us cultivators! We become one with our fields and our soil, only to be born again. Do we abandon this event that sustains us for the entire year? Do we reject this new life?

My mind was not ready.

The talk about the strike was spreading. Newspapers were writing about it. Many sarpanches passed resolutions in villages around Puntambe. The momentum was building. Somebody needed to give a formal statement about the strike to the government. Dr Dhananjay Dhanavate from Puntambe took the lead and reached Mumbai along with a few friends. He is known to be a supporter of Radhakrishna Vikhe Patil, the then leader of opposition in the Assembly. He went through Vikhe Patil, who took the group to meet Chief Minister Devendra Fadnavis. CM Fadnavis knows his game well. He leaves you enthralled with his speech. And as the delegation came, how could he spare that opportunity? He accepted the statement and, in principle, agreed to the demands. Now, as the demands were met, though, in principle, there was no need for a strike. The Chief Minister convinced the delegation that the strike was over even before it started. And, obviously, he made sure that the media covered this.

Meanwhile, as in any other village, Puntambe too had rival political groups. When the news spread that Vikhe supporters had called off the strike, another leader Dhananjay Jadhav, known to be a supporter of Snehalata Kolhe, entered the scene. People condemned those who had called off the strike and made a strong resolve to continue with it. A state-level preparatory meeting was organized in Puntambe on 22 May 2017.

3

During all this, I had just returned to my native place Akole, in Ahmednagar district. Kisan Sabha had taken out an *Asud morcha* (whipcord march) on the then agriculture minister, Pandurang Fundkar's house. Our demands were complete freedom from debt, MSP, land entitlement, facilities for irrigation, functional PDS, and rural health services. I had been travelling across the state to mobilize for this march, and it was a grand success. This agitation had helped us bring the demand for freedom from debt back on the table.

I was exhausted after this month-long mobilization for the march. I needed to rest at least for a week. Working in my hospital was almost like that rest. I could sit in my cabin, check my patients, and order tea as and when I wanted. And then, have friends like Chandrakant Bhot and Shantaram Gaje over, chat, discuss all things under the sun, including the latest books and what people were reading. If there was free time, then take a book and just read to my heart's content. This was pure leisure. I had not been to my clinic in so many days. My wife, Dr Archana, was managing everything on her own. She managed the house and also the hospital. To add to that, she would have to spend sleepless nights when a patient went into labour. And what was I doing? Mobilizing and protesting, for the last 19 years, almost imprisoning her to the rut.

I did feel guilty, but that too was convenient, I guess – typical of a man.

So, there I was, planning a break.

It was nine in the morning, and I had just reached my clinic. Nilesh, Rohidas and Khandubaba arrived.

'The farmers' strike is making news,' said Rohidas.

'Yes,' I replied.

'They have a meeting tomorrow in Puntamaba,' Khandubaba said.

'So?'

'So, we should go there,' Rohidas stated.

'We . . . ?'

All of us burst into a laugh.

I knew they had a plan.

'And what about my break?' I asked.

Another round of laughter.

There are some friends you can't say no to. These three are such. I had received a call from Vitthal More, a senior Kisan Sabha leader from Latur, suggesting that I should go and visit Puntambe. And I was anyway curious about the strike. So, finally, we decided to attend the meeting planned at Puntambe on 22 May. We left early in the morning to reach in time.

We reached at 10 am, covering a distance of 80 kilometres. Puntambe town is spread along the railway line and has a population of 17,000. This area is rain-fed, dotted with a few irrigated farms. Dairy is an additional source of income. The place is famous for Asha Kendra, a health centre treating paralytic patients. Nothing much, otherwise.

The news of the strike and now this statewide meeting had suddenly brought Puntambe into the limelight.

The meeting was yet to start. So, I decided to take a stroll. I parked my car on the campus of Asha Kendra. Dr Dhananjay Dhanavate works as the Chief Administrator of the centre.

Paralytic patients from all over the state visit the centre and stay for two months. The centre is famous for its effective care and thus is always crowded. Today was no different. Hundreds of people with paralytic bodies and deformed faces were dragging themselves to the centre with the help of their loved ones. The air was filled with a kind of bitter sadness.

This was Puntambe – famous for treating people rendered inadequate by paralysis.

Was it just these people, or was it the entire countryside with its farming and farmers that were paralysed? While cities basking in glory swelled by each passing day.

So, Puntambe was famous for treating paralysis.

Let's see . . .!

The meeting was organized in a spacious hall outside the Changdev Maharaj temple. Not many people had arrived, and the number of farmers barely touched hundred and twenty-five, that too after waiting for some time. I was whiling away my time and was, in fact, quite bored.

Finally, the meeting began at one pm. Dhananjay Jadhav, Jayaji Suryavanshi, Sandip Gidde, Suhas Vahadane were on the stage. We were in the audience, listening to their speeches. The organizers would undoubtedly do with some organizing skills, I thought. Nothing was in order.

I was meeting Jayaji Suryavanshi for the first time. He has recently emerged as a farmers' leader. He was the only one who looked keen and active. He kept interrupting the speakers now and then with some suggestions. He reminded me of those bubbly and boisterous young girls in any wedding who are all over the place. But, nobody really seemed very serious about the meeting. One after the other, leaders continued with their campaign like speeches. I had no choice but to sit and watch.

I was asked to speak towards the end. It was quite late, and the meeting had lost its steam. I was in no mood to speak, but I had to. I began by admiring everyone for mooting the idea of the strike. But I also shared my hesitation about the idea of 'no sowing/cultivation' as I felt it was impractical to do so. For me, not supplying produce to the market was much more practical than appealing to people not to cultivate. Cutting off the supply of fresh produce to the cities was more 'practical', I said, withholding the farm produce, depriving the cities, and thus trapping the government – that would be a better strategy. I was trying to find the middle path, and a few of them responded to it – just a few.

The meeting was over. The only takeaway was that the farmers were going on a strike.

Why? How? Against whom? With whom? Not much got planned.

O' Changdev (save them)!

4

The agrarian crisis had caught the farmers in a deadly trap. The government had stopped responding to the traditional forms of protest. The agitation had to get creative. And the strike was indeed an attractive idea. But it was a two-edged sword, and we needed to be careful. Much was discussed, but some issues were still unclear. For example, the direction it should take, its outcome, planning, preparations, mobilization, expanse, intensity, and a possible response – all needed some clarity. When bank officers, petrol pump managers, doctors or teachers go on a strike, we know what they would do. We also know what the repercussions are. We know who should take note of the strike and for what reasons. There is an ideological and theoretical clarity. There was no such clarity about the farmers' strike yet.

What does it mean when farmers go on a strike? Whom are they protesting against? And why should those, who are protesting, be concerned about it? Most importantly, the farmers have to unite without any factions to go on a strike. How do we achieve that? Many such questions needed meaningful answers, not emotional responses. Unlike the industry, agriculture does not have clear cut divisions between an owner and a worker. The farmer bears a double burden of being an owner and a worker simultaneously. He also runs a dual risk. The production relationship in agriculture is quite complex. A farmer cannot pressure someone else by not working on their own farm. Also, a farmer has an emotional bond with farming. There is an organic union between a farming family and agriculture. So, deciding not to cultivate one's land is not as simple as giving prior notice about the strike and shut shop.

Cultivating for one's own needs was suggested to solve this complex issue of farmers' strikes. It was argued that a shortage of farm produce would bring attention to the demands. But it was conveniently ignored that importing these goods was an option. Besides that, farmers do have necessities that go beyond food. And to suffice those, they need money, in cash. Where will that money come from if one does not sell the produce? Nobody answered this question. That is why not cultivating as a form of the strike was non-practical.

Instead, the strike would succeed only if we refused fresh farm produce to the cities. We needed a plan to stop the supply of fresh items such as milk, vegetables, leafy greens, chillies, curry leaves, etc. That would make it more effective. It was necessary to prevent any supply from other states. Though, I don't think anyone seriously thought about this in the Puntambe meeting. The meeting was over, and we came out.

The meeting was held outside the old temple of lord Changdev.[1] People believe that this yogi lived for 1400 years. Gracefully riding a tiger, holding a snake in his hand, he was almost smiling. I thought all of us have one Changdev (one who is arrogant) within and outside us. What we lacked was Muktai (a guru to guide and liberate).

---

[1] Changdev was a Nathpanthi poet and yogi. His image is used here based on his interaction with saint Dnyaneshwar.

'She will appear only with experience,' Khandubaba tried to pacify me.

We left. Both of us had not eaten since morning. We were pretty worried and a little depressed, too. We continued our journey.

'One place near Sangamner Phata, serves good *misal*, with curd,' Khandubaba suggested.

We stopped there and ordered a *misal*. It did not taste as good. Anyway, we let it be.

5

The farmers will go on a strike! The newspapers carried the headline the next day. The confusion created by 'in principle' promises by the CM was no longer there. The meeting did achieve this. Now we needed to work towards making this strike more practical. I organized a meeting at the Rest House in Akole and called my friends and fellow travellers. I spoke with all those I met at Puntambe and some new leaders working under the banner of Kisan Kranti. I wrote an article in the daily *Lokmat*. We started receiving a good response, and we hoped that all the groups would finally reach an agreement.

It was proposed to do a sit-in satyagraha in Puntambe beginning 25 May 2017 to help spread the word across the state. We also needed a centre to coordinate the strike. This satyagraha could help us with that, and it could also build momentum. We could iron out the differences during this period and reach an agreement. The proposal made sense.

So, on 25 May, we were again going to Puntambe. This time Nilesh and Rohidas joined us. The idea of the strike was fantastic, but due to inexperienced leadership, the planning was not spot on. Kisan Sabha needed to be involved so that it would be more organized. And, it so happened that Dr Ashok Dhawale, a central leader of Kisan Sabha, was visiting Nashik the same day. I was keen that he should come and start the satyagraha at Puntambe. It could have been the best way for Kisan Sabha to get involved. I knew that he supported all good initiatives. So, when I asked him, he agreed to come.

A pandal had been set up near the main road in Puntambe. It could accommodate not more than 200 people. Around a hundred farmers from the surrounding villages had arrived. The satyagraha was, to begin with, the lighting of the lamp on the stage.

Sandip Gidde had arrived a day before. I was curious to know more about him for his expertise in organizing the Agri-Exhibitions. He said he had a vast database of farmers through these exhibitions and the social media data from the Maratha Kranti Morcha. He claimed that using these data, he would publicize the strike across the state in his own style.

When we arrived, BJP leader Dhananjay Jadhav and Suhas Vahadane met us. Soon, Dr Dhawale, Kisan Gujar, leader of the state council of AIKS; Anil Ghanwat, leader of Sharad Joshi-led Shetkari Sanghatana; Giridhar Patil; Seema Narode; and others arrived.

The local BJP MLA Snehalata Kolhe visited the pandal and had a chat with the protestors. But she did not stay till the inauguration. Why didn't she?

Anyway, that's how it goes.

Soon, the programme started. Dhananjay Jadhav welcomed everyone and explained the background of this day. Then two girls who had come to support their father's strike gave speeches.

In recent times, it was as if the entire generation of young girls was on strike, and the fathers stood in their support – just like the Dhagya[2] mountains, rock-solid. 'I am ready to marry even a *sihpai* (police constable), but not a farmer', was their slogan. They went on a strike against 'agri-culture', rejecting farming, farmers and the entire countryside – desolate and miserable. They had seen their

---

[2] Dhagya is a mountain range surrounding Akole town.

mothers, sisters and sisters-in-law spend their whole lives in this hell called farming. These girls refused to enter that hell.

They were right.

It was a blood-sucking hell. One that denies you the dignity of human life.

The programme continued. People came and lit the lamp – the satyagraha began. Speakers shared their thoughts. But I was getting sucked into a deep, endless black hole.

Deep down.

With me came hordes of young unmarried men. Down to the bottom, deep in the hell.

Farming has turned into hell, my friend!

Speeches continued. Leaders kept saying that farming was a loss-making business and the government policies were deadly for farmers. They spoke about these unmarried youngsters and how they are heading towards radicalization. This would put not just the cities but the entire society in danger. There will be unrest and anarchy, they claimed. Nobody was safe.

I could imagine some stones being hurled at me.

Baap re! (Oh dear!)

This seems dangerous.

Really? Is no one safe here? Is that so?

'Doctor, come, let's have lunch,' Rohidas called, and I came out of that trance.

The farming crisis is simmering like a volcano. It is boiling in the minds of our youngsters. What if that volcano erupts?

It is frightening!

Anyway.

Some leaders had spoken, and some were to speak post-lunch. Villagers had organized food. All of us ate in the pandal. The rest of the speakers shared their thoughts, and the programme ended. Overall, it went well.

Good!

Meanwhile, the issue of 'not cultivating land' died down. It was decided that from 1 June 2017, we won't supply vegetables, milk, and fresh farm produce to the cities. We would cut off the food supply and trap the government. This was how the strike would be.

Good!

Social media had played a crucial role in the Maratha agitations. Some of us were active on numerous Whatsapp groups on *Sakal Maratha*. There were many sympathizers in news channels and print media. Through all these contacts, efforts were underway to spread the word about the strike. We decided that few activists would join the sit-in in Puntambe, and the rest would travel across the state organizing meetings and public gatherings. Everyone was gearing up for 1 June.

6

So, the farmers were really going on a strike.

But, what was their exact motive?

Two months ago, an hour before CM Fadnavis was to address a gathering in Mul in Chandrapur district. Umed Chaykate, a farmer from Bhadurni, 8 km away from Mul, ended his life. He was under debt. Here in Mul, the CM talked about the troubles faced by farmers and there in Bhadurni, Umed Chaykate's lifeless body hung from a tamarind tree. As police were busy providing security to the CM, the dead body could not be removed for the next four hours. Even death could not end the disgrace.

Umed Chaykate was not an exception. Farmers were ending their lives each passing day. Young children were untying the noose and bringing down the bodies of their loved ones – fathers and brothers. Every village was counting dead bodies every day. Shivba's Maharashtra was turning into a graveyard for farmers.

Umed died. Panchanama was done. Investigations followed. They were able to find the reason behind the suicide. After much effort, the system came out with a convincing fact. For them, Umed was not a farmer. So, they did not need to worry or bother as this was not a 'farmer's suicide' case. And even if it was, there was not much to worry about.

For this thick-skinned bureaucracy, this is not unusual.

Umed Chaykate laboured to feed his family. His younger brother cultivated their ancestral farmland. Umed's family did not own any land in his name. There was no loan against the land that his brother cultivated. Umed Chaykate was not a farmer. The state cared a damn.

Umed's story is not an exception. According to the official data from the department of revenue and rehabilitation, Maharashtra witnessed 20,873 farmer suicides from 2001 to 2015. Of these, 10,390 suicides were declared ineligible for compensation. The main reason was these farmers did not have land in their name – just like Umed.

Now, why did they not own any land? The reasons were worrisome. The situation was dreadful, reminding us of Umed's face and his lifeless body hanging on a tamarind tree.

In the state, with each generation, the farmland got divided. The size of landholding per household kept decreasing. According to the 1970-71 Census, in Maharashtra, on average, each farming household owned 4.28 hectares of land, reduced to 1.45 hectares in 2011. With each passing day, the landholding size is shrinking. The farmland was reduced to tiny pieces of land, and it was impossible to do any productive farming in that land. It was not enough even to feed a family. This was the case with at least 75 per cent of farming households in the state. More and more farmers were becoming landless, completely decimated. The villages were turning desolate.

The economic indicators of this misery in the countryside were alarming. Our policies have been corporate and urban-centric. They are favourable neither to the farmers and farming nor landless rural labour. As a result, there is absolutely no 'net income' in agriculture. The only yield is loss. The farmers just didn't earn any 'net income' whatsoever.

Such income could have supported that brother who moved out to lead his own life if there was such income. It could have averted this land division and resulting misery of the villages. It could have created more employment and sustained more people. But, the yield from the farm does not even help recover the cost of production. Neither does it help repay the farm loan. It only puts the next generation in debt and pushes them towards farm labour. This is how the farmers have ended up on this downward spiral.

Over many generations.

This downfall is rooted in how we view farming. We consider farming a self-supported occupation that provides raw material to the nation, industry, and government schemes. We assume as if those working in agriculture are legally in bondage.

Bonded labourers that we are entitled to!

We conveniently forget that those who put in this hard labour also have needs. And that they have to make savings to fulfil those needs. To date, all the governments have time and again intervened in the market and have reduced prices of the farm produce. This is to appease the industry, processing units and exporters, consumers who are voters and their donors, resulting in the loot of farmers, farming and fields.

Farmers have lost their ability to cope with disasters such as drought. And thus, it is the state government policies that are responsible for the loot and indebtedness of the farmers. The government has to accept it.

It has to own its responsibility. One can do this by returning the loot, if not entirely, at least partially, and this can be done by waiving off the loans. Policies that value and remunerate farmers' labour will ensure that the farmers do not fall into the debt trap again. We also need alternative agricultural plans and programmes that revive farming, regenerate soil, and bring the countryside from misery and destruction.

These were the main demands of the proposed strike by farmers.

So, the farmers were going on a strike. The sit-in had begun in Puntambe. The preparations for the 1 June strike were in full throttle.

7

I was very keen that Kisan Sabha put all its force behind the strike. Over the last two years, Kisan Sabha had engaged in agitations and had emerged as a force to reckon with. On 29 and 30 March 2016, it had organized a massive protest by farmers in the CBS square in Nashik. More than one lakh farmers stayed put in the square for the *Mahamukkam satyagraha* (mega sit-in satyagraha). In Aurangabad, farmers from Marathwada had organized *Shetkari akrosh satyagraha* (Farmers' cry satyagraha) at the collector's office. On 30 May 2016, Thane witnessed a huge *Tirdi*[3] *Morcha* where anti-farmer state policies were put on the *tirdi*, ready for cremation. On 3 and 4 October, 50,000 Adivasi farmers reached Wada to gherao the then Tribal Development minister, Vishnu Sawra, to bring attention to their plight. The *Mahagherao satyagraha* was successful. On 11 May 2017, farmers from over 22 districts, after a month-long mobilization, carried out an *Asud morcha* on the residence of the then agriculture minister, Pandurang Fundkar. Kisan Sabha has been a prominent farmers' union that successfully mobilized many farmers for these agitations. All these efforts would surely help the strike get a large number of farmers onto the streets.

The main issue was that the rest of the farmers' unions looked at agriculture from a market-centric view. But Kisan Sabha constantly analyzed farming comprehensively and advocated for alternative policies for comprehensive and dynamic development of agriculture. It strived for equitable and sustainable development of all sections of the countryside. It was aware that development

---

[3] *Tirdi* is a plank to carry a dead body for final rites, made of bamboo sticks.

does not entail the destruction of biodiversity and the environment for earning profit. Kisan Sabha always put its faith in public policies that promote sustainability and happiness in human life. It looked at agriculture from such a broad perspective. And that is why I thought that Kisan Sabha needed to play a pivotal role in the strike.

8

All this while something was important was happening for the farmers' struggle. On 22 May 2017, Raju Shetty, a Swabhimani Shetkari Sanghatana MP, started an *aatmaklesh* (penance) rally from Mahatma Phule Wada (Mahatma Phule's Residence) in Pune.

In 2014, Shetty had fought the Lok Sabha elections under the leadership of Narendra Modi. He had campaigned hard to put BJP in power in the state and at the centre. He had put all his might into this. BJP too paid back Swabhimani by giving them some berths in the government. Sadabhau Khot, considered the right hand of Raju Shetty, was made state minister of agriculture. Ravikant Tupkar was made the chairman of the Textile Corporation.

As time passed by, Raju Shetty and Sadabhau Khot drifted apart. It is said that it was BJP behind this drift. When things reached a dead end, Raju Shetty decided that Sadabhau should step down. Sadabhau refused. This made things worse. In the end, Raju Shetty started opposing the BJP. He said that he made a mistake by supporting BJP in the Lok Sabha elections, and now as a penance, he will walk from Pune to Mumbai.

Shetty was confident that the BJP government would bow down to his act, Sadabhau would be asked to leave, and CM will come and meet him when he reached Mumbai. But nothing happened. The CM ignored Shetty's penance and got Sadabhau closer to his camp. He schemed to break the Shetty-Khot friendship, which in turn would weaken the farmers' struggle.

The CM did one more thing to divert people's attention from Shetty's agitation. Shetty had planned to culminate his rally in

Mumbai on 30 May 2017, and the CM chose the same day to send Sadabhau Khot, the then state minister of agriculture, to Puntambe. There, Khot announced that he had come with a meeting proposal from the CM. This ensured that the media shifted its focus from Shetty to Puntambe. It was a clever ploy – ignore Shetty and focus on Puntambe. Raju Shetty was not in the news, and the not so known Puntambe was making headlines. And in a bid to sideline Shetty, the government inadvertently spread the news of strikes across the state.

9

On 1 June 2017, the phone's ringing woke me up at 4.30 in the morning. I was exhausted after the daylong meetings and the journey back. I spoke to many Kisan Sabha activists across the state. Abhijit Kamble called me in the afternoon. A TV channel was organizing a debate on the strike. Nikhil Wagle had invited me to Mumbai to participate in the debate. It was important to take part as it would help spread the word. Sandip Gidde, Shankar Darekar, and I represented Kisan Kranti. It took 5-6 hours to drive to Mumbai. The panel discussion was quite useful. It helped get the message of the strike across to the farming families. Now, the strike was indeed a statewide event.

I had to return to Akole after the programme got over. We needed to be stationed in the village on 1 June, when the strike was to begin. I reached Akole around 3.30 am. Khandubaba was with me as always. We spent the night at our Hospital. As I was just about to sleep, the phone rang. I was tired, but that call made me forget everything. I was thrilled. Someone from a far off village in Solapur district had called. He said, 'Doctor, we have blocked our main road at 4.30 am. All the youth are here together. We have stopped the vehicles carrying milk and vegetables, and we will make sure that not a single vehicle moves from here. Please do not backtrack now.'

And the phone just kept ringing with calls from Nashik, Ahmednagar, and Pune. Now there was no doubt in my mind. Young farmers, even outside any union, were out on the roads. Khandubaba had a great time listening to those calls. By 6 am, it was clear that the strike was in full swing in Nagar, Nashik, and Pune. News channels covered the near-empty APMCs. The strike had begun. Educated youth from the farming community was now in control of the strike. How could I sleep now? In a hurry, I got ready and began my day.

This was simply good!

By noon, the strike had gained ground. News of blocked roads and stranded vehicles started flowing in from nooks and corners of the state. Farmers knew about the strike, so they had not harvested the produce and vehicles belonging to the traders were being stopped midway. The milk vans too were blocked, and thus, by evening, the milk collection would stop. The milk collection centres, the federations and dairies were requested to co-operate. A few APMCs closed down today; the rest would follow tomorrow. The cities, including Mumbai, would now feel the pinch.

And the point was precisely that – they'd been compelled to respond.

Bravo!

10

I visited the APMCs on 1 June, appealing to them to down the shutters. And Dr Dhawale called. He asked me about the strike. He was happy with the developments and wanted all the unions to join hands. The party had organized a study circle on 2 June at Adarsh High school in Mumbai. Many leaders from sister organizations were going to attend that, and the veteran leader of the CPI (M), Sitaram Yechury, would address the group. This was a golden opportunity to discuss the strike and get Kisan Sabha to participate. Dr Dhawale asked me to reach Mumbai as soon as possible. I was in Mumbai the day before, had reached Akole at 3.30 in the morning, and had begun my day in an hour. And now Dr Dhawale wanted me back in Mumbai. I was tired and sleepless. But there was no other way. So in the afternoon, I left for Mumbai along with Khandubaba.

I spent the night at Janashakti – the CPI(M) office in Worli. Cotton mills and workers' colonies once surrounded the area. It was a thriving centre of the workers' movement. And now, the mills have shut down, and tall, high-rise towers have taken over. The rich live here and work in their posh, air-conditioned offices. The sirens indicating the change of shifts have died down, and so have the gate meetings. Where did the workers go? The senior comrades say they have gone – 'far-away'. How far, no one knows. The despair in their eyes is disturbing. Now, in some occasional rally by the mill workers, one hears a muted and sluggish demand for 'Housing for mill workers'.

This is called development! Cruel and terrifying.

I spend hours looking at photos on the office walls. These are our senior comrades. Their eyes share a dream of a just and happy place. I converse with that dream for many hours.

I tell you, it is not very easy to pursue one's dreams and keep yearning to reach a destination far away. And to keep at it over generations and to get up and chant – 'We shall overcome . . . ' after every defeat . . . it is tough, my friend.

Is it indeed so?

Not for those who seek that eternal joy. For them, it is not that difficult.

I called Rohidas early in the morning. I had not been able to contact anyone while travelling. So, I had asked Rohidas to keep in touch and get updates from everywhere. I was relieved. In Vitha Ghat in Akole, young farmers had blocked vehicles transporting vegetables. The milk supply, too, was blocked. Similarly, in Kotul, vehicles transporting farm produce were stopped. Rohidas Dhumal, Nilesh Talekar, and Dr Sandip Kadlag were making every effort for the strike to succeed. Anil Dethe and Santosh Wadekar from Bhumiputra Shetkari Sanghatana were active in Parner. Residents of Puntambe came out in huge numbers. Anil Ghanwat from Shetkari Sanghatana actively monitored the activities in Ahmednagar and surrounding areas. News from Nashik and Pune was promising. So, in all, the situation was hopeful. And now, I was to talk to the study circle participants about the strike. I wanted to garner their support.

We reached the camp in much excitement. The hall was jam-packed. Comrade Sitaram Yechury was expected any moment. The idea of a farmer going on a strike was in itself novel. The audience had leaders and activists who have led hundreds of successful strikes. Their appreciation showed on their faces. The atmosphere in the hall was full of life. I shared the idea behind the strike, its demands, and the response it received. I updated them about the current status of the strike, and I appealed to them that all unions of workers, students, youth and women should come out in support of the strike. People were so thrilled that the hall was filled with cheers and slogans before I could even end my speech. When Sitaram Yechury arrived, the hall was resonant with slogans of unity of workers and farmers. The farmers' strike had got overwhelming support.

Bravo!

Someone proposed that Sitaram Yechury should immediately address a press conference to spread this message of unity and fraternity across the state. Dr Ashok Dhawale consulted him and got his nod. Shailesh Kamble went ahead with preparations. As soon as Sitaram Yechury's presentation was over, all of us, the office-bearers of Kisan Sabha, headed to the press conference. Comrade Yechury enquired about the strike and was quite happy to know the developments. Anyway, he is always cheerful and seeking happiness. I think true comrades are always happy . . . always.

All of us reached the venue sharp at two o'clock with Sitaram

Yechury. The press conference was at Mumbai Press Club, just next to the Azad Maidan. A large number of journalists attended the conference as they were pretty curious about the idea of the strike. This was the first time they were covering a strike by farmers. We kept repeating that young farmers from numerous villages were leading this strike. Kisan Sabha was in support. Comrade Yechury and Dr Dhawale announced that all unions were supporting the strike. And to demonstrate that, all the unions affiliated with the Party (CPI(M)) were going to participate in the Maharashtra bandh (a statewide strike) planned on 5 June.

11

The press conference was over at 3.30 pm, and we were on our way out. We wanted this strike to reach across the state, and for that, the next two to three days, we needed to work ceaselessly, seriously, and patiently. 5 June was a statewide Maharashtra bandh, and we wanted it to be a grand success. The next three days would surely test how mature our leadership was. We kept discussing these issues and things looked fine.

And, suddenly, we got this phone call from Puntambe, which completely took us off guard. The CM had called the coordination committee for talks. Sandip Gidde and Dhananjay Jadhav had announced their decision to meet the CM on the news channels.

How could this happen? How?

What happened to the unity and the collective decision making? Or trust? Nothing mattered, is it?

Why this haste?

The CM had played another game, not letting the strike spread. This was a clever move.

We had returned from the press conference around 4 pm. Khandubaba insisted that I eat something, as we had not had any food since morning. I was in no mood to eat after that phone call. I immediately called Gidde, who was busy giving soundbites to the news channels. He didn't answer my call. Dhananjay Jadhav, too. I then called Shantaram Kunjir from the Maratha agitations. He was in Pune and claimed that he did not have any clue about the invitation for talks. Anil Ghanwat from Shetkari Sanghatana was clueless, too. We expected that such decisions would be made only after discussions and deliberations. But it seemed that some of us were thrilled to get an invitation directly from the CM. For them, it did not matter if they took all of us in confidence or not. I kept trying their numbers but in vain. I could not get in touch with Gidde, Jadhav, or Darekar.

At last, Gidde called back and shared the invitation for talks.

'We are reaching there tonight, and we have already announced that. We are on our way,' he announced it in one go. 'We will meet in Mumbai. You are anyway there,' he disconnected. He seemed extremely busy with the news channels.

It was impossible to lead a statewide strike without getting everyone on board. This was damaging for our unity. It seems that our dear friends happily forgot everything about unity in the noisy din of the media.

12

I was trying to call each and everyone from the coordination committee. For many, it was not possible to immediately reach Mumbai. I called Gidde and told him that talking to the CM would not be right without getting everyone on board.

'Get tomorrow's appointment so that we can send out the message to everyone. We can sit down and decide our strategy. We can decide which demands to push for. And most importantly, we can also decide when and on what grounds shall we stop any further discussions. The strike would have got some more momentum, and that will put pressure on the government to accede to some more demands.' I was trying my best to convince Gidde.

But he was a man of words with a ready answer. He said,

'Doctor, the CM is not in Mumbai tomorrow. So if any discussion is to happen, it is tonight. Please don't worry. Let us go and discuss at least. We will not call off the strike unless we get a nod from everyone. We will only discuss. Our decision can be conveyed later. Anyway, you are in Mumbai. Let us meet tonight around 11 pm at Varsha (CM's residence). We are on our way. Jayaji Suryavanshi is with us. Shantaram Kunjir is reaching. Anil Ghanwat is not able to make it, but Seema Narode will represent the Shetkari Sanghatana. Don't you worry. We will set everything right.' Gidde seemed super confident.

I messaged Dr Ashok Dhawale regarding the CM's invitation for talks and asked if I should go. He gave his nod saying that one of us needed to be there. So, as soon as the panel discussion was over, I headed towards Varsha along with Khandubaba. We had not eaten anything in the afternoon, and now we did not want to get late, so we skipped dinner as well. We reached Varsha at 11 pm. I parked my car. The tea stalls had shut for the day. The roads were not very busy, and there was a routine police presence. One does not see many pedestrians here anyway. No other crowd. Both of us sat on a roadside bench, and I called up Gidde one more time.

'Doctor, the meeting has been cancelled. The Secretary is not available at this hour. So if anything is to happen, it is only tomorrow. You do not need to wait at Varsha. I will give you a call tomorrow.' He hung up.

Is it so?

My heart sank. Something was amiss. We just sat on that bench in the darkness of the night.

After fifteen minutes, I called up Darekar, who always came with Gidde. I knew that Gidde and him had travelled in separate vehicles today. I asked him where he had reached.

'We are about to reach Mumbai. Sadabhau has invited us for dinner. Join us,' Darekar told me.

'But what about the meeting?' I asked.

'Let's have dinner first. We are meeting after that,' Darekar said.

My guess was correct. It seemed that Gidde did not want me in the meeting. Now, there was no turning back. Khandubaba found half a packet of biscuits in our car. He gave me two, and we sat that at the roadside, waiting. And as luck would have it, a ripe mango fell off the tree above. Both of us happily shared it. And we kept waiting. I rang up Gidde. 'I heard you are having dinner at Sadabhau's. Is that true?' I asked him directly.

'Yes, all of us are hungry. You are welcome. Let's eat together,' Gidde said.

This wasn't very good.

'The entire state, on our call, is out on roads on strike. Sadabhau is a minister in the government. I suggest that you should avoid this dinner at his residence. It will land you in a soup,' I pleaded with him. But he seemed to care a damn. He had lost it. Reason did not work at all.

The night progressed. We were sitting on the bench outside Varsha. Images of young farmers on strike kept playing in my mind. It was getting quite dark.

Gloomy and dim.

13

The roads glistened in the milky white street light. There was a nip in the air and an eerie silence, the kind from the graveyard, unrelenting. A second seemed like ages. We were patiently waiting. I thought to myself, this kind of wait takes away time from one's life, and one heads towards death.

Utterly disgusting!

We kept waiting. The night passed by.

We were anxious, worried, fed up, agitated . . .

Helpless and waiting . . .

For the leaders of the strike.

And around 12-12.30, there came a cavalcade of cars which turned towards Varsha. Their headlights lit up the road. We blinked. The reporters were waiting at the entrance. The protestors followed police vehicles and stopped there. Protestors got down. Their caps had 'Farmers on strike from 1 June' printed in green. The police was identifying each person. They let in those on the list. My name was there, and Khandubaba's was included on the spot. We were led to a Meeting Hall. Sandip Gidde sat in the first row. Jayaji Suryvanshi got himself space beside the CM. Khandubaba, Kunjir, Satish Kanawade from Sangamner, and I sat together. The CM entered the hall quietly and conscious of his steps. Sadabhau Khot and Chandrakant Patil accompanied him. MLA Snehalata Kolhe rushed in. The discussion began.

Sandip Gidde briefly shared the background of the strike. 'We had a very fruitful discussion with Sadabhau over the last one and half hours. We are here to discuss some other issues,' Gidde announced.

He started with ideas on how to make the farmers self-reliant. Gidde and Suryavanshi took turns while discussing this issue. Sadabhau intervened a few times, and the CM looked interested. Chandrakant Patil sat there, unaffected, pretending to smile. Ten-fifteen minutes were spent discussing this. But nobody broached the topic of the loan waiver. Finally, I intervened. I kept my cool and participated in the discussion.

'Farmers across the state are on strike for two important demands, a loan waiver and minimum support price for their crops. So I request that these demands be discussed,' I appealed.

'Doctor, that loan waiver business is done with. In principle, the government has agreed to it. Sadabhau has told us just now. So the demand actually ceases to exist,' Gidde announced.

I was shocked to hear this. If it was so, why are the farmers on strike then?

Gidde was speaking in the CM's language. They were clearly influenced.

'Sandiprao, in-principle loan waiver means nothing if there is no clarity on who will benefit, the amount of loan, and when will they waive it,' I asserted and maintained that the discussion should centre on these points.

As I spoke, the CM started getting restless. He was keen to come in now.

'My friends, in principle, we have agreed to the loan waiver. So the question is over. We will implement it at the right time. Let us not discuss it now. I think the discussion should now focus on ways of enabling the farmers to stand on their own feet.' The CM spoke in a high pitch.

Every time the demand for loan waiver came up, this was the position CM took. He always agreed but only 'in principle'. For the last two years, he had refused to share when he would implement it. His standard answer was that he would roll it out at the right time. The farmers were on strike because they wanted to know when exactly was the 'right time'. There was nothing new in agreeing to the loan waiver unless a timeline was mentioned. This cannot be considered a victory of the strike. If the loan waiver was not implemented on the ground, the strike would prove futile.

It seemed that no one from the delegation cared. In fact, they got busy canvassing for their projects submitted to various government departments, as these were crucial for making farmers self-reliant. The discussion went on.

Machiavelli's assertion that desire for individual gain is always more potent than morality and ethics seems, in this case, to be true to the tee!

14

I let time pass, and after fifteen-twenty minutes, I again intervened. 'Unless we tell the farmers who will benefit from loan waivers how much is the amount and when it will happen, we cannot ask them to call off the strike. So we should discuss these critical issues,' I insisted.

The CM was irritated with me and wished I was not there.

'My friend, I did say that the issue was done and over. We have, in principle, agreed to the demand. Let us not keep repeating it now', the CM said angrily.

I was a little surprised by his aggression. For a moment, I forgot that it was the CM talking. He was agitated, and at that moment, Gidde came forward.

'We need to make farmers self-reliant, and that is more important than the loan waiver. Rather than discussing that, why are you stuck on the loan waiver, Doctor? Why waste time?' Gidde asked the golden question.

Now, I was getting agitated. It was 2 am. The meeting was going in a different direction. I was convinced that it was all set up. I tried to explain it to Shantaram Kunjir and Satish Kanavade. They seemed to agree but chose not to say a word. Gidde, Jayaji, and Darekar just went on and on. Dhananjay Jadhav too added to the discussion.

After a while, I again intervened. 'Respected Chief Minister, we need to discuss how we can announce your proposal to the people. So I suggest that we meet in the adjoining room to discuss this. We will get back to you with our collective decision.' I tried one last time to get a chance to discuss this with the delegation members.

The CM did not want to give me any such opportunity. 'Ajitrao, those who cannot convince people about their decision do not make good leaders. Let it be any decision; we should be able to make people agree to it. There will always be some naysayers. Why bother about them?' The CM gave a valuable suggestion!

We have seen the CM doing precisely this. Be it the Maratha agitations, Dhangar agitations, or the farmers' agitation. He has been convincing people to agree on anything while he has not bothered his critiques. At times, he has very skilfully 'managed' those from his clan or the outsiders. He has mastered this art.

But what happened to us? We, like fools, still keep our faith in principles, commitment, truth, honesty, democracy, etc.

All rubbish!

But still, I refused to backtrack. I forced Kunjir, Kanavade and Darekar to come along with me to the next room. Gidde, Jadhav, and Jayaji did not leave the hall. After a while, Jayaji was sent in to see what we were up to. I tried my best to convince my colleagues that the CM was fooling us. 'If we call off the strike and do not have any concrete decision on loan waiver in hand, the farmers will never forgive us. This 'in principle' does not mean anything. We cannot go back now until we get a concrete decision in our hands.' I was trying my best to convince them.

Some of them did seem to agree with me but were not willing to support me openly. Jayaji, Gidde, Jadhav, and Darekar were hell-bent on calling off the strike. This would be like backstabbing my young farmers. I often felt that my colleagues were not mature enough, but I started doubting their integrity today. They were obsessed with making the farmers 'self-reliant'.

I agree. The farmers needed to stand on their feet. But it was also essential to stop this loot, to get back what has been looted for generations. The loan waiver is a way of returning this loot.

But no one was bothered. All of them had left, leaving me alone in that room. A deep sense of loneliness filled me from within. And it is a terrible feeling to be left alone to review the possibilities and responsibilities on your own. That is why people prefer to be in a mob, follow others and even think as a mob mindlessly.

So, there I was, all alone.

I returned to the meeting hall. The preaching on how the government was helping farmers to be self-reliant was still on.

I was alone, within and outside.

15

The picture was becoming more evident now. But I did not give up.

One more proposal. Was it a new trick to pass the time, or was it to cover their treachery?

I intervened again. I said, 'I will not object if you all feel that the discussion is positive. But I have one request. Let us finish our discussions here, but the decision to call off the strike should be announced in Puntambe after taking everyone in confidence.'

'No way!' The CM was shouting. Before I could finish, he got up and said, 'You should just stop it now! We will see what to tell Puntambe's people. Snehalata tai (sister) is here; she will take care of it.' He was now visibly irritated.

Dhananjay Jadhav seemed to agree with me. In a soft voice, he repeated what I said. He said it was wise to make the decision in Puntambe. But he was under a lot of pressure as I saw Snehalata tai get up from her place and come to Dhananjay Jadhav to tell him something as if to convince him. Jadhav glanced at me and then looked down. It was getting more and more difficult for me to talk to Jadhav and Darekar. As a last resort, I messaged Darekar and Jadhav, 'Trust me, do not make any final decision here. Get everyone in confidence in Puntambe and then only decide.' Both of them looked at me after reading that, and again, looked the other way.

I took a big risk and loudly said: 'People will not spare us. This is a wrong decision'!

I could sense the tension in the room. Gidde was very angry. He got up. Looking at me, he said, 'I am the one who has started this game! And Doctor, I know how long it will last. If we continue the strike tomorrow, it will be the farmers who will end it. So, please, stop it now!' Gidde said in a decisive tone.

Impossible! I could no longer save them from people's anger. I had exhausted all efforts to keep our unity intact.

I sat there. Silent.

It was past 3 am. Khandubaba went out of the hall to stretch his legs. It was him and me on one side and the rest on the other.

The decision was in their favour. Jayaji was ecstatic. He seemed like a hunter with a big catch. Outside, the Press was waiting. Here, people were ready to pose for cameras.

The images were important to none other than Jayaji.

16

I was repulsed and did not want to stay there even for a minute. But at the same time, I could not get myself to leave. I could not abandon my fellow travellers. I knew that people would pounce on them when they realized that they had not gained anything. I was familiar with the politics of Puntambe. Dhananjay Jadhav's opponents were waiting for the wrong move. When Vikhe was mediating, Jadhav had created a lot of noise on how he backtracked without much gain. And by maligning the Vikhe camp, he had taken the reign of the strike in his hand. Now it was his turn to face the heat from the Vikhe camp.

Meanwhile, police had used brute force on farmers and their young ones. One of them died of a heart attack while on the run. Many were booked under arson. Any decision to call off the strike without any concrete promise will not go down well with them. The media, journalists and many intellectuals were supporting the strike. They, too, will not like it if any decision was made casually, without any deliberation. I could see that all those hailing our agitating farmers would not spare them at all.

And most importantly, any loss of trust in the mind of farmers was detrimental to future protests. Will they ever trust us again? This would be a massive blow for the agrarian movement.

For me, it was a catch-22 situation. If I supported my colleagues, I was an equal partner in the sin. And if I left at this moment, I would betray my fellow travellers. And I was representing Kisan Sabha. If my reading proved wrong, there was no coming back for Kisan Sabha in this entire struggle. My mind was racing. Khandubaba kept telling me to have tea. I couldn't.

But, it always happens when in crisis, until I calm down. And there I realized that I was calm. It was a sign that I had made up my mind. Once again, I looked at everyone. I got up, came out of the hall, and called Dr Dhawale. It was 3.30 am. Still, he answered my phone immediately. I was relieved. Any decision to boycott this meeting could not be made by me alone. I needed to confirm it with him. I briefed him on what happened and how others were managed. 'I needed to talk to you to confirm that my reading is not wrong. I do not wish to continue with the meeting. And I seriously want us out of this sin. What do I do?' I asked him.

'What do you feel like doing?' he asked.

'Comrade, I strongly feel that we should boycott this meeting and leave. And, we should appeal to our farmers to continue with the strike,' I shared my opinion.

Without wasting any time, Dr Dhawale backed my decision. I was pretty relieved. The burden came off. And I was happy that I was on the right path. I went back to the hall calmly. I told Khandubaba what we decided. 'You stay back. Just observe what happens. As soon as I call, you come out. Do not waste any time . . .!' He nodded. I stood up and looked at everyone. I announced in a clear, loud voice, 'Friends, I cannot support you in this decision. Forgive me for that. I am leaving.'

Their reactions did not matter to me now. The press was waiting outside the gate. My decision of boycotting the meeting had to be shared before the decision to call off the strike was announced. Otherwise, it would lose its impact. I had to meet the Press before CM got them. I was racing.

17

It was 4 am when I came out of the meeting. I was struggling to reach the gate. In the dark, I was not able to find my way. The entry door we used earlier was closed. The police were signalling. But I was stuck, just like a wild animal in a cage. I kept coming back to the meeting hall. Time was precious. I had to tell the entire state how the CM had backstabbed us. But I just could not find my way out. It was frightening.

One young policeman was watching me. He had seen me present the farmers' issues in the meeting. He said something to his fellow policeman and signalled me to follow him. I had no other option but to trust. I followed him as he took me down using stairs as the main door was locked. If he waylaid me now, the game was over. 'Please take me to the gate where the press is waiting. It is very, very important,' I pleaded with him. His eyes twinkled. I came out of the door, and it was bright and lit. He stayed back in the darkness. He pointed to the left and said, 'Dada, I too am a farmer's son!' He turned his back and walked off. I was overwhelmed.

In four big strides, I reached the gate. 'Let me out,' I requested the police. Numerous press reporters were waiting with pen and paper in their hands and a few cameras. They were going towards the gate as the CM had called them in.

'I was in the meeting. Most of the farmers' leaders have turned traitors. I have boycotted the meeting and left. I need to give a statement on behalf of the Kisan Sabha,' I said in an audible voice.

Many reporters had covered comrade Sitaram's speech in the afternoon. They knew me. Some were, of course, too keen to meet the CM.

'This will break the agitation and harm movement. Don't you think so?' one concerned reporter asked.

'Take this on record. Mark my words as I am convinced that my decision is in the interest of the farmers. I want to bust the CM and also the traitors.' I stood my ground.

Everyone just stopped after hearing this. The cameras rolled. My statement was getting recorded and with it the fact that I was no longer part of this betrayal. There was tension. But inside, I was calm. The news channels were recording my statement. Reporters were making notes. This was going to send shockwaves across the state.

'I represented Kisan Sabha in the meeting called by the CM. His only agenda in the entire discussion was to end the strike, misleading other members of our delegation. He has not agreed to our demand for a complete loan waiver. He is fooling us with his evasive responses of willingness for "in principle" agreement with the loan waiver.

'It is up to others if they want to go ahead and call off the strike on the basis of these non-committal responses. But this is cheating. It is vague and does not commit anything concrete to the farmers. So, Kisan Sabha is appealing to the farmers all over the state to continue with the strike. We should not step back unless our demand for a complete loan waiver is met. Our peaceful protest should continue, and Kisan Sabha stands firmly with the farmers in this.

'This protest began in Puntambe, where the Gram Sabha passed a resolution that they will not back off until and unless a complete loan waiver is announced. I feel that those negotiating with the CM right now are deceiving the farmers of Puntambe.

'Many organizations in the state have supported the strike. These include unions of farmers and workers. Kisan Sabha will not support any move to call off the strike without discussing it with these unions.

'We are appealing to the people of the state to continue the strike. Till our demand for a complete loan waiver is met and recommendations of the Swaminathan Commission are implemented, we should not take a step back. Kisan Sabha is requesting all of you.'

I presented my case to the media.

I could sense some disquiet among the reporters. Some clearly seemed to sympathize. And once again, I was convinced that I was right. I called Khandubaba and told him to come out as soon as the meeting got over. I started going towards my car. I had an inclination that things could take an ugly turn. I felt that I should wait here till the press came out. I called Dr Dhawale and narrated what all happened. I asked him if I should wait outside. 'Don't even think of that. Anything can happen. You two should just leave and reach Janashakti in Worli. We will decide about this tomorrow,' he spoke in clear words, more as a command, but from a place of concern. I sat in the car and called Khandubaba to make it quick. The gates were open for the press to come out, which helped him. We left immediately.

But it was not over. We did not know the way out. Earlier GPS had helped us, but now there was no signal. Half an hour passed; we were lost. Finally, some men collecting ripe mangoes fallen from the trees showed us the way out. We reached Janashakti by dawn.

II

18

I had not eaten anything the day before and had not slept in the night. As soon as I laid down in the Janashakti office, I fell fast asleep. In half an hour, Rohidas called: 'The media has presented both the sides. Our stand is correct,' Rohidas was excited.

Fantastic!

I felt much relieved. Within five minutes, I received a call from TV9, a news channel: 'Will you be on the panel for the 7 am show?' There was no question of saying no. We had to send the message across the state and present our case. I quickly got up, got ready and left for the studio. TV channels had started giving news that the strike was called off by that time. The media were busy covering how APMCs had opened their shutters.

Pramod Chunchuwar had joined me in the discussion on a TV9 show. He began to speak, and the anchor said, 'The CM has agreed to the loan waiver in principle. He has also promised to write off loans of marginal farmers. Then, why do you still need the strike?'

'The CM did agree "in principle" to waive the loan. But he had declared that he would need to study who would benefit and how much loan to waive. And this would take some time, he said. Every day farmers are ending their lives. And the CM is delaying to act under the garb of a study. It seems like he wants to time it with elections. Any delay will cause more suicides. That is how stark the situation is. And again, he is talking about marginal farmers alone. The most vulnerable farmers from Marathwada and Vidarbha have bigger landholding but meagre yields. If the waiver is restricted to

73

marginal farmers, then these farmers from rainfed areas are not going to benefit. Also, the CM does not announce any concrete plan. It's all very vague and subjective. It was out of the question that we agree to such conditions when the strike is on,' I explained our stand. Chunchuwar came in my support. The discussion took a favourable turn. I was delighted. As I was leaving the studio, other news channels started calling. I had decided that though it was pretty hectic, I would not refuse anyone. It was necessary to put out our position as quickly as possible. Half a cup of tea later, we were on our way to the next studio.

Meanwhile, I had asked Rohidas and Nilesh to go to the Nashik APMC. They had reached there in the morning to ensure that it remained shut. They called me at around 9 am. After a meeting in the APMC, a decision was made to down the shutters. The strike was on. News channels started reporting that the strike was still on. Rohidas felt that it was essential to hold a meeting the next day in the Nashik APMC. I asked him to contact Sunil Malusare and Raju Desale. Both immediately started off to Nashik to prepare for the meeting.

Soon, Raju Desale called. 'We are planning a meeting. Sunil Malusare is with us. You must come.' That phone call was a great relief. The strike needed a new centre, and Nashik emerged as the right option. I told them that I would reach. The evening news was all about these unforeseen events in the strike. Nikhil Wagle on TV9, Ashish Jadhav on Maharashtra One, and Sanjay Awate on Saam invited me for a panel discussion.

The news channels played the prime-time debate promos throughout the day. With that was a photo of the CM whispering into Jayaji Suryavanshi's ears, with the caption: what did the CM say to Jayaji?

Using the picture was an intelligent move.

It was a historic image!

It was used widely to imply or suggest that Jayaji was hand in glove with the CM. It was circulating on numerous social media groups.

Who clicked it, really?

And who gave it to the media?

Jayajirao, the power-hungry politicians, are no one's friends!

19

Now, we needed to begin afresh. We could not build trust unless all the important farmer's organizations were on board. I had said this, right at the outset, in Puntambe. The organizers in Nashik had invited Budhajirao Mulik to address the gathering. If all the significant farmers' unions, intellectuals working on farm issues, progressive farmers, writers, and journalists came together on a common platform, it would build our strength.

And along with that, it will also help in creating confidence. The events of the last night required us to put more effort into building trust. I started working on it.

I knew many farm leaders, and I started calling them up. In past, Kisan Sabha had organized few agitations along with Raghunath Patil faction of Shetkari Sanghatana. Balasaheb Patare from Ahmednagar and Kalidas Apet from Beed were his lead men. I spoke with both of them and also with Raghunath Patil. He said he would leave from Sangli and promised to be there for the meeting at Nashik.

Then I called Anil Ghanvat from the Sharad Joshi faction of Shetkari Sanghatana and invited him for the meeting. Surprisingly Ghanvat termed the demands incorrect. 'Asking for a loan waiver is nothing but begging. And so is the demand for a minimum support price. Why should the government make decisions regarding farm prices? The state should give us freedom of market and technology, that's it. Farmers will then price their produce. Our main demand should be the implementation of the Martial

75

Plan designed by Sharad Joshi. We, in the Sharad Joshi faction of Shetkari Sanghatana, cannot participate in any protest with such demands and asks for alms,' Ghanvat said.

This was ironic as Ghanvat was with us in Puntambe at the onset of the strike and had shared the same stage. He had played an active role in blocking the vehicles carrying farm produce in and around Ahmednagar. He had also shared that a case had been filed against his son for the same act. On 2 June, Seema Narode participated in the meeting representing their organization. All this while, the demands were not 'begging'. What happened now?

'Come for the meeting in Nashik. We will discuss the demands. I really hope you can make it. All these young farmers relied on us and are out on strike. We cannot step back midway,' I tried to reason with him. And it worked. He agreed to come.

I was not getting through Bachchu Kadu. I requested Dr Dhawale to invite Raju Shetty. He called back and said, 'I spoke with Raju Shetty. His feet are swollen after the *aatmaklesh* agitation. So, he is resting and can't make it to Nashik. He also feels that the events of the previous night have put a blot on the strike. So, we should wrap up and take a break. Later, with renewed energy, we should start afresh,' Dr Dhawale said.

I felt sad.

Kisan Sabha had always felt an affinity with Vijay Javandhiya's positions. He, too, said that the timing was not right. 'No one in Vidarbha will come out on roads as people are busy sowing. What am I supposed to do alone?' He shared his inability to attend the meeting. I contacted some intellectuals from Sharad Joshi's protests. Many of them felt that the timing was not right. They shared that we should take this opportunity and wait for the right time and come out stronger.

Barring a few, most of the people shared this opinion. But, our resolve was firm. The last few days had helped us peep into the minds of these young farmers.

There was no doubt that we were right. We just needed to stay calm and build a broad consensus. I knew from my heart that the Nashik protests would prove to be a turning point.

20

It was 4 June. I left Nashik to reach Mumbai for a meeting. On my way, I stopped at Adarsh Vidyalaya. The hall was packed to its capacity. Everyone was upbeat about how we intervened last night. They looked keen but also worried. Dr Dhawale suggested that I should update everyone on the current status of the strike and our role in it. I spoke for ten minutes.

'The fight is no longer only of farmers. All of us must join hands. All this while, these educated, aware youngsters have watched how their farmer parents were being looted. They are on strike across the state. We should put all our energies behind them. See, this workshop will be over today, but tomorrow, as we go back, we should be out on roads with all our might,' I made a sincere appeal.

Dr Dhawale and Kisan Gujar spoke in my support. Cheers, claps, and slogans in the hall gave me goosebumps. The sound kept ringing in my ears, even on my way back to Nashik.

Leaving behind the life-sucking crowds of Mumbai, we were heading towards Nashik. The phone kept ringing. I just couldn't afford to miss a single call. The calls were non-stop, a few from journalist friends but mostly from young farmers from different villages.

'Doctor, come what may do not backtrack. We are there to support you,' they were pleading.

21

It was 10 am when I reached Nashik. Farmers had started coming into the APMC. The stage was being set up, and flex banners were up. Raju Desale and Sunil Malusare came and told me that MLA Jeeva Pandu Gavit was expected. I could see many activists busy with the preparations. Those included Amruta Pawar, Chandrakant Bankar, Chetan Shelar, Darshan Patil, Ganesh Kadam, Gangadhar Nikhade, Hansraj Wadgule, Kailas Khandbahale, Karan Gaykar, Madhuri Bhadane, Nana Bachhav, Prakash Chavan, Prabhakar Waychale, and others. I was happy to see Sharad Deshmukh and Ashok Arote of Shetkari Sanghatana. Rohidas and Nilesh, too, had returned from home in the morning. Khandubaba was with me. I could see some 2000 to 2500 farmers who had gathered for the programme, and that was just enough to spread the message that the strike was still on. It was announced that only farm leaders should be on the stage. Many local MPs and MLAs were in the audience to avoid any political overtone. The gathering started off with fire. Budhajirao Mulik was elected as a chair. Giridhar Patil of Shetkari Sanghatana was sitting by his side. Raju Desale welcomed everyone and started the speeches. After two other leaders spoke, it was my turn. The farmers were cheering and in high spirits. Everyone was firm on continuing the strike. Many news channels were broadcasting the event live. This was the most opportune moment to broadcast the message of strike all across the state. I thanked all my farmer brothers and sisters and began with my speech.

'This is a golden moment in the history of the agrarian movement in India. And you are creating that history. The young generation of the farmers from across the state is looking up to you with hope. You have organized this gathering and have taken a stand to promote the strike. I thank you on behalf of those millions of farmers who have been battling the crisis. Hearty congratulations!'

People began to cheer and clap even before I could finish. Their sloganeering filled the venue. One could sense the excitement of the crowd. I briefly presented the strike's background and how the CM tried to scuttle it on the early morning of 3 June. I prepared to give the final blow:

'The CM has succeeded in blowing up the strike at Puntambe. On this backdrop, who will lead the strike, people ask. It will be the educated young farmers who will lead it!' (Thundering applause and cheers).

'Educated and aware youngsters who have realized the how their parents were looted and dispossessed . . . they will lead the strike. That young generation will successfully lead the strike now!' (Another round of applause and cheers)

'The historical moment in the strike, the most important event will be the Maharashtra bandh on 5 June! That is going to be a pivotal event.

'So, my friends, Do not think far. Do not worry about how many days the strike will be on or whether we will do *rasta roko* or even a rail roko. Just don't think! Use all the tools and means you have; count on your friends and relatives across the state and your own families. We are not going to limit ourselves to Nashik alone. Now we have our eyes set on the entire state! Make it such a massive success that Fadnavis (Maharashtra CM) will have to come running here!' (Massive applause and cheers)

The speech delivered its effect. The news channels broadcast this speech to every corner of the state. Hundreds of cell phones got active. The video clip went viral on Whatsapp and Facebook. The preparations for the Maharashtra bandh were in full swing. The gathering in Nashik played a crucial role in the success of the strike.

22

It was necessary that all leaders sat together and made further plans. Varsha Pawar arranged the hall in the neighbouring bank, with much effort, for the meeting. MLA Gavit participated in the gathering, but he could not stay back. So, he left. Sunil Malusare from Kisan Sabha was there. As soon as the keys arrived, we opened the first-floor hall and went in. It was almost 5 in the evening, and the hall was quite crowded. It would have been difficult to conduct any business, so Raju Desale stepped in and announced, 'Each organization will have only one representative. All others kindly leave the hall.' This did not go down well with a few, and they started to argue. Some others began quarrelling with us. But we kept our cool, and soon we could commence our discussions. Budhajirao Mulik had left after his speech in the gathering.

The discussion was serious and focused. Meanwhile, Raghunath Patil arrived. Everyone had agreed that we needed to form a new coordination committee, as the earlier Samanvay Samiti was now defunct. It was agreed that each organization should nominate one member. The first name announced was Raghunath Patil. And the second was Raju Shetty's. The moment he heard it, he jumped from his chair and said, 'Impossible. If this is how it is, here I leave!' He got up to go.

I knew that Raghunath Patil and Raju Shetty were not on good terms, but I never realized that there was so much bitterness. The entire plan was falling apart. Hansraj Wadgule from Swabhimani Shetkari Sanghatana stood his ground and pushed for Shetty's nomination. All the leaders stated that it would not be possible to plan and implement the strike without getting the prominent leaders involved. So people pacified Raghunath Patil. Soon, he agreed and sat in his chair. Now we were looking for a third member. And that was Bachchu Kadu.

After a lot of discussions, a draft list was prepared which had the following names: Ajit Navle, Anil Ghanwat, Bachchu Kadu, Chandrakant Bankar, Eknath Bankar, Ganesh Jagtap, Ganesh Kadam, Giridhar Patil, Hansraj Wadgule, Bhai Jayant Patil, Karan Gaykar, Raghunath Patil, Raju Desale, Raju Shetty, Sanjay Ghatnekar, Santosh Wadekar, and Shivaji Nandkhele. It was decided to include Budhajirao Mulik, Chandrakant Wankhede, Vijay Javandhia, and think tank. Darshan Patil, Nana Bachchhav, and Prakash Chavan had managed the social media during the Strike. So it was decided to put them in charge this time as well.

The earlier committee was called Samanvay Samiti. We decided to take a new name with a unique identity to avoid confusion. We should function as *Sukanu Samiti* (Steering Committee), I proposed, and all agreed. It came up during discussions that we need someone to coordinate with all. Giridhar Patil suggested my name for the role. Everyone agreed. This is how Sukanu Samiti was formed. Later in the strike, these words carried a lot of weight. I was elected a State coordinator of the Sukanu Samiti.

23

The formation of Sukanu Samiti provided a new pivotal centre for the strike. The news channels and media helped spread the news across the state. The statewide bandh would help in intensifying the strike. All of us were now geared towards making the bandh a grand success. All branches of Kisan Sabha were actively working for this. I knew that if we received good support for this, then many farmers' organizations, leaders, and political parties would come in support of the strike. Many activists of Kisan Sabha too agreed to this.

'Win this fight on 5 June, and the victory will be yours!' Our campaign for the bandh centred around this slogan. Young farmers across the state were now in action. The deceitful action of the state to crush the strike had hurt them the most. Social media was full of campaigns for making this bandh a success.

Maharashtra had recently witnessed a storm of Maratha Morchas. The Maratha community had taken out 52 rallies, with up to 20 lakh people attending some of them. The leaders of Maratha Morcha understood that the condition of farmers belonging to this community had its roots in decaying agriculture. That is why along with their other demands, the Morcha had included farming-related demands such as the implementation of the Swaminathan Commission recommendations and MSP for farm produce which is equivalent to the cost of production plus 50 per cent and a loan waiver. These Morchas played a massive role in building a base for farmers' strikes. The Fadnavis government was yet to fulfil the demands of the Maratha community. The educated youth of this community were angry. And now, when they saw how the state tried to cheat them during the strike. Determined to make the strike successful, the youth did everything they could.

Congress and Nationalist Congress Party had campaigned throughout the state on the issue of loan waivers. They had also voiced their concerns regarding this issue in the assembly. But the government did not pay any heed. So, they too saw a golden opportunity to canvas their issues through the strike.

All is not well between BJP and Shiv Sena recently. Since the BJP assumed power, they had demeaned the Sena in every possible way. This strike provided Sena with the much-needed opportunity to get back at BJP. We thought it wouldn't officially support the strike but would get its grassroots cadre to participate. Our entire focus was on the young farmers in the countryside. There was not a grain of doubt that they would come out on the streets.

The message from Nashik was loud and clear: the Strike was on. Now we needed to do the same from Puntambe. Maharashtra bandh would allow us to organize a public meeting and spread the same. Dr Dhanvate had agreed to organize this. But we needed to make sure that the village level politics was kept out of this. People had promised that they would not let that happen. Puntambe was readying itself for the meeting.

24

The atmosphere on the day of the strike was unforgettable. The strike had gone beyond Nashik, Ahmednagar and Pune and reached other parts of the state. The News channels covered the events of the Maharashtra bandh right from the morning. The farmers were out on the streets, and roads were being blocked.

And it was so spontaneous that leaders-activists from all political parties barring the BJP had participated in the strike.

Along with Khandubaba, I had reached Akole the previous night. In the morning, we left for Puntambe. Rohidas was with us. We wanted to reach as early as possible to avoid getting stuck in the *rasta roko.* Still, after 8 am, we started facing blockades and had to change our route quite often. Village after village, people were out on the streets. I was happy to see this response.

After much effort, at around noon, we somehow managed to reach Puntambe. The earlier pandal which was built for the sit-in organized by the Samnvay Samiti was now dismantled. A new one stood in front of the Gram Panchayat for the meeting organized by the Sukanu Samiti. Farmers from the neighbouring villages had arrived in significant numbers. The villagers had decided to take out a rally before the meeting. They had made an appeal: As much as possible, walk barefoot to condemn the act of deceit by the state government. Khandubaba, Rohidas joined me, and we started walking barefoot on that scorching tar road. Lalusheth Dalavi, district president of the Maratha Mahasangh, had come from Ahmednagar. He, too, joined us. Many people took out their shoes and chappals and started walking behind us. We walked through the village almost for an hour. The road was blistering hot, but the farmers kept walking. This act of penance was mighty. It achieved what it aimed. The meeting began. Speakers appealed to everyone to join hands and start the strike in unity. No one criticized anyone. That was the need of the hour.

The News channels had daylong coverage of the meeting, the strike, its impact, and analytical discussions by intellectuals. I could participate in many panel discussions on various channels from Shirdi. Through that, I could advocate our position, demands and the future direction of this struggle. The bandh was successful. Those who had faulted us on the strike's timing were now praising it. Those sitting on the fence or the ones in hiding now came out in the open and supported it. The strike was being steered in the right direction.

25

During the farmers' strike, roads were blocked in many places to stop the supply of farm produces to cities. Farmers stopped vehicles carrying vegetables and milk. Vegetables were strewn on streets, and milk cans were emptied. Farmers expressed their anger through these acts. Maharashtra bandh protests on 5 June saw many such incidents across the state. The middle class criticized this. The pro-government brigade opened its tirade on social media. They claimed that this product was 'food' and any wastage of this food was an insult to the divine, Parabrahma.

For years, when market prices crashed, this divine food was thrown away in the market, in gutters, on the road. They never saw that as waste. Why?

And what about when we go to the market and use all our 'capital intellect' and 'inherent skills' to bargain and further bring down the throwaway price of this divine food? For us, the value of our farmer's labour is counted in a rupee or two. At that moment, do we ever think that we are devaluing this divine food? Why is that?

My friend, why ask such scathing questions?

Fine, I won't!

The fact is that none of us backed this idea of throwing away the produce. It was painful to watch it thrown on the roads, as we knew what it takes to grow it. The farmers, too, were pained. It was as if they had thrown themselves on the roads – agitated, helpless, and angry.

Karl Marx put forward an excellent theory: alienation. One must read his analysis of the process of production. Marx says that a worker puts himself, his persona, in his creation.

So, a worker or a craftsman puts his persona into things that he 'creates'. He puts himself in that. Marx says that a worker looks at his own reflection into what he creates.

What about the farmer?

Is it the same with the farmer? Does he look at his own reflection into his produce? Does he see himself, his inner reflection, in his produce, creation, and crop? Which for others is divine Parabrahma, is it 'Swabrahma' for a farmer? When his produce sells at a throwaway price, does he get this unsettling feeling that his own self is worthless? Fallen market prices, the feeling of being helpless and worthless in the international market, the overall process of globalization has led farmers into being alone and lonely and into a financial trap. Are these at the root of farmers' suicides? Do you think that the demand for a fair price for farm produce is inherently linked to ensuring fair and just treatment to our farmers?

Why ask such difficult questions, my friend? Be fair. Make it easier.

Alright.

So, going back to the strike, many roads in different areas were blocked to cut the supply of fresh farm produce to the cities. Farmers expressed their anger by throwing vegetables on the roads and emptying milk vans. The farmer's strike had reached all corners of the state.

26

Maharashtra bandh on 5 June was a grand success. We were happy that the state did not witness any violence. We had always maintained that ours would be a peaceful protest. The state government and the police, too, were acting with restraint. The farmers had blocked the movement of goods. Numerous vehicles carrying vegetables and milk were stopped midway, and the produce was thrown on the roads. So many farmers were booked for dacoity and violating lockdown. Some were arrested. But still, there was no violence.

Inspired by the events in Maharashtra, farmers from Mandsaur in Madhya Pradesh went on a strike. They tried to cut supplies to the cities. But, the Madhya Pradesh government responded with bullets. Six farmers were killed and many injured. We were troubled to hear that.

Farmers in Maharashtra were watching how their produce was going to waste, and still, the government was not paying any heed. They were on edge. It was feared that the Mandsaur episode would repeat here. The lives of farmers were valuable. We needed to make the right decision.

Right after the Maharashtra bandh, on 6 June, we had planned to gherao the tehsil offices. On 7 June, we had announced our plan to protest at the residence of our ministers. But, what after 7 June? We had no answers. People were suggesting that we should organize a more comprehensive conference of farmers and then decide. Now, it was possible to do it in Nashik.

27

It was collectively decided that on 8 June we will organize a conference at Nashik. Local organizations agreed to support it. I reached Nashik on 7 June evening with Khandubaba. We oversaw arrangements at the venue. A meeting of the Sukanu Samiti was planned at 10 am, and the decisions of this meeting were to be announced at the conference. We were keen that all the leaders of the farmers' movement attend the meeting as well as the conference. Raju Shetty was yet to confirm. I knew that Bhausaheb Chaskar, a proactive teacher and a journalist from Akole, was close to Shetty. I once again sent the invite to Shetty via Chaskar. That seemed to be working.

The events that were unfolding were reminiscent of the Sharad

Joshi-era. The Nashik conference was going to be similar. All those who were connected with the agrarian movement were watching out. I had never witnessed such a vibe. It was charged and ecstatic.

The Sukanu Samiti was organized in the Rest House. Most of the leaders reached on time, and the meeting began. Many people who were not members of the Samiti wanted to join the meeting, and many were requesting an entry. We would have liked everyone to join. Most of the prominent names from the farmers' movement were there. Dr Ashok Dhawale, Bachchu Kadu, Bhai Jayant Patil, Raghunath Patil, Raju Shetty, and all other members of the Sukanu Samiti were present. The news about the meeting was being aired on all news channels. Everybody was looking forward to the next step of this protest. Many reporters from Marathi and the English press were there at the venue. The entire state seemed to be with Sukanu Samiti.

The word *sukanu* (or steering) has its deep roots in the movement. Akole block has a rich history of the Independence struggle and the Communist-Socialist movement. I have seen these movements in their prime. The leaders from both movements would come together in various protests. And to co-ordinate within themselves, they would form a committee. These were called Sukanu Samiti (Steering Committee) most of the time. Later, the movements died down, and these Sukanu Samitis literally lost their name. The word was forgotten. This strike revived it. People would ask what *sukanu* meant. Many possibly did not know its meaning. A *sukanu* is a mechanism that steers the ship on the seawaters in the right direction. People understood when we used the term steering. It was a perfect word. It was a golden word. We needed nothing but steering to get the strike, deliberately waylaid, on its right path. The strike had got its steering.

28

We began the meeting. Dr Dhawale suggested that I should

87

update everyone on the ongoing protests. Bhai Jayant Patil seconded him. I gave a brief update and put forward the agenda for this meeting.

The farmers went on a strike by cutting the supply of farm produce to cities. They have been at it for the last seven days and incurred huge losses. In the beginning, we had decided on the seven day- period. Some people stated that if the government did not pay any heed to our demands, then we should go on an indefinite strike. I, too, pointed out the same as the need of the hour.

There were many other proposals. Some suggested that the prominent farm leaders sit on a hunger strike on Azaz Maidan in Mumbai. The others were protests at the ministerial residences or a march of one lakh farmers to Mumbai. All the proposals were thoroughly discussed. In the end, we decided to do a rail roko across the state.

This was the right call as it would take the strike to other states. Farmers from Madhya Pradesh, Karnataka, and Punjab were agitating and came out on roads. Kisan Sabha had very recently led successful protests of Maha Paadav and Chakka Jaam. Farmers from Madhya Pradesh took inspiration from their counterparts in Maharashtra and went on a strike. Those in Uttar Pradesh were agitated due to the deceit in the loan waiver scheme. Farmers across the nation were watching the events here in Maharashtra. A rail roko would stop transport to other states and give an opportune moment for farmers in those states to protest and come out in the streets. What began in Maharashtra could now spread to the entire country. The BJP did not want nationwide protests at any cost, which would put the central government in a very tight spot. Everyone was confident that a rail roko at this moment was the right decision. So, we decided that we would wait till 12 June for any response from the government. And if there were none, from 13 June onwards, we would go on an indefinite rail roko and stop all interstate rail transport. This would give us an opportunity to take our protests across the country. In a unanimous decision, I was told to share this decision of the Sukanu Samiti at the farmers' conference.

29

The conference venue, Toopsakhare Lawns, was close to the rest house in Nashik. A large number of farmers were reaching the venue. Police had made unprecedented bandobast. When we arrived at the venue, the hall was bursting to its brim. We had to move chairs in the front row twice to vacate space and accommodate more people. Finally, the organizers pushed back chairs and put up a new pandal on the lawn outside the hall. That, too, was full in no time. The response of farmers was unprecedented. Many new leaders and organizations were present.

Along with those, many veteran leaders from the agrarian movement made it a point to attend. It was important to take cognisance of that and to accommodate all different streams in the movement into the steering committee. We had prepared forms for documenting information of organizations and their leaders attending the conference and also of those willing to be part of the steering committee. More than two hundred and fifty organizations showed their willingness to join the Sukanu Samiti. We were amazed by the response.

So many prominent farm leaders were present in the hall that we found it impossible to get all of them on the stage. Hundreds of media reporters and their camerapersons thronged the place in front of the stage. The conference was being broadcast live. Something like this had never happened in the history of the farmers' movement. I started my introductory speech after everyone was welcomed and the chair of the conference was selected. I was there to share the decisions of the Sukanu Samiti.

I congratulated everyone for making the strike and the Maharashtra bandh a grand success. 'We have successfully completed the first phase of seven days where we cut the supply of fresh farm produce to the cities. Now we enter the second phase of the protest. In the first phase, we only cut the supply of farm produce to the cities. But now, to make the state accede to our demands, we will block the transport fully. We would not step back even if we had to bring to a halt the entire country. Need be, we will lock down the entire nation for the cause of farmers. So, as the first step of this protest, Sukanu Samiti has decided to do a state wide rail roko on 13 June.' Thus, I shared the decision of the Sukanu Samiti, and the farmers welcomed it with a roaring cheer.

'The Sukanu Samiti is giving this government time till 12 June to fulfil our demands. If it doesn't respond to us by that date, then on 13 June, hundreds and lakhs of farmers will come out and sit on the rail tracks. Not alone, they will come with their young ones and their cattle. They will stay put on the tracks. Prepare yourselves for a do or die protest from 13 June, which will be remembered as a milestone in the history of the farmers' movement. And we will not restrict ourselves to Maharashtra alone. The protests will now go to other states. The Sukanu Samiti has made this decision in today's meeting. The farmers across the state will not stop till the government kneels. I appeal to all of you to support this decision and create history. Join this struggle to free your farmer parents with all your might.'

I tried to be brief in presenting the future direction of the protests. The decision was welcome with a loud cheer and sloganeering. Everyone agreed that the rail roko was the right decision. The enthusiasm was palpable.

After this, the senior leaders addressed the farmers. It was the first time that all prominent leaders in the farmers' movement shared the stage. The conference had created hope. Dr Ashok Dhawale, MLA Bachchu Kadu, Bhai Jayant Patil, Raghunath Patil, Raju Desale, and MP Raju Shetty raised important points in their speeches. I wanted more people to speak. I tried to accommodate more leaders from farmers' unions and asked senior leaders to wait. We could not give time to some of these leaders, which upset them, and later some of them stayed away from the protests organized by Sukanu Samiti. The conference had time constraints, so it was inevitable. Most of the news channels broadcast this event live, and it reached every household in the state. National media took it across to other states. The press also covered the conference widely. All this had a significant impact on the government.

30

In the beginning, the rulers did take the strike very lightly. They thought they would wind it up by getting a few people on their side. They also believed that the farmers would not bear the losses as the sale of their produce was blocked, and everything would collapse. They also thought the strike would go haywire, as no one face [led the strike]. But nothing happened. The formation of Sukanu Samiti and the success of the Maharashtra bandh brought made the protests more organized.

The government had also changed its stance. The chief minister claimed that those leading the strike were not 'real' farmers. He had said, 'We are ready for any discussion with genuine farmers. But, we will not speak with the bogus ones.' He was, of course, pointing at me. His perception that I was not a farmer was not only wrong but also laughable. He was trying to trivialize the agitation by neglect, disdain, and creating false impressions.

All this turned around after the Nashik conference. A decision to get into rail roko created opportunities for taking these protests across the country. And this could put none other than Prime Minister Modi in a tight spot. And the CM could no way afford to lose Modi's confidence. He was starting to lose his guard. The Nashik conference had hit a bull's eye, and the CM could no longer neglect the protests. The government had to initiate discussions with the Sukanu Samiti the next day. They had to call a 'bogus' farmer like me and invite him for a meeting. A meeting was organized on 11 June at Sahyadri Guest House in Mumbai. A five-member high power committee was set up. It included the revenue minister Chandrakant Patil, agriculture minister Pandurang Fundkar, minister for water resources Girish Mahajan, minister for transport Divakar Rawate, and minister for co-operatives, Subhash Deshmukh.

They were compelled to take this action.

31

The fallout of the Nashik conference was that more than two hundred and fifty organizations were now willing to work with the Sukanu Samiti. We were trying to get new leaders and their mass organizations to work with the already active members of the Sukanu Samiti. It was necessary to decide points for discussion and which members would participate in the meeting with the government. We needed to finalize these things a day before the meeting. So the third meeting of Sukanu Samiti was planned for 10 June at the Shetkari Kamgar Paksha's (PWP) party office at Mahim in Mumbai. As the state coordinator, I formally invited all the committee members and a select few from the new organizations willing to work with us.

Khandubaba, Nilesh, Rohidas, and I reached Mumbai on the night of 9 June. We spent the night at Janashakti. We called each and everyone and requested them to come for the meeting. The Nashik group had made great efforts for the conference, so we were very keen to participate. I called up Giridhar Patil at 11.30 pm and suggested that all the activists book a vehicle and come together for the meeting. Patil said that he was looking after that. All the preparations were complete, and I was feeling relieved.

But, peace and relief are always momentary. What lasts long is anxiety. The next day morning brought this back to me.

News channels were running the news that the Sukanu

Samiti had split. Giridhar Patil had announced his decision of not attending the meeting, claiming that there was no need to talk to the government while the agitations were on. A few hours before, he was all set to reach Mumbai, and through the night, he had changed his mind. I was completely taken aback. Testing times were not yet over.

I had great respect for Giridhar Patil. I was a regular reader of his newspaper articles. We had been together in this since the sit-in at Puntambe. In fact, he was the one who had wholeheartedly proposed my name for co-ordinator of Sukanu Samiti. He was trying to get the Nashik team here. What happened then? His position had put us in a tight spot. People started talking about the split in the campaign. Media reporters had started visiting Janashakti to get my reaction on this.

If our protest was to create a nuisance, there was no need to talk to the government. But if we sincerely wanted to resolve the issues faced by farmers, then the discussion was critical. At this juncture, it was essential to keep up the pressure and get the demands fulfilled through concrete talks. We did not need protests that yielded nothing. Farmers had borne huge losses over the last week. How could we not seriously discuss their demands and only get into some stunts?

The farmers' strike, Maharashtra bandh and the Nashik conference had put pressure on the government. We had increased it by announcing a rail roko. The state had no other option but to concede to the farmers' demands. Howsoever reluctant, they had to invite Sukanu Samiti for discussing the issues. And in such a situation, not participating in the meeting was, for me, suicidal. 'Sukanu Samiti will not take any detrimental decision to the protests. We will meet at Shekapa (PWP) office at 12.30, and then at 4 pm, we will address a press conference. We will announce our delegation at that time,' as a coordinator, I was sharing our position with the media. Inside, I was hurt by Giridhar Patil's stand.

On 10 June, Dr Dhawale, Khandubaba, Rohidas Dhumal, Nilesh Talekar, and I reached the PWP office early in the morning. The media reporters had arrived even before us. Bhai Jayant Patil, Bhai S. V. Jadhav, Raju Korade and other PWP activists made all the arrangements.

As the state co-ordinator, I had formally invited Anil Dethe, Anil Ghanwat, Dr Ashok Dhawale, Bachchu Kadu, former Chief Justice B. G. Kolase Patil, Balasaheb Chavan, Chandrakant Bankar, Chetan Shelar, Darshan Patil, Devand Pawar, Eknath Bankar, Ganesh Jagtap, Ganesh Kadam, Giridhar Patil, Hansraj Wadgule, Bhai Jayant Patil, Jyotsna Vispute, Karan Gaykar, Khandu Wakchoure, Kisan Gujar, Namdev Gavade, Nana Bachchhav, Prakash Chavan, Raju Desale, Raju Shetty, Raghunath Patil, Rohidas Dhumal, Sanjay Ghatnekar, Sanju Bhor, Santosh Wadekar, S. B. Patil, Shivaji Nandkhele, Vijay Javandhia, Vishwas Utagi, Vishwanath Patil, and Vitthal Pawar.

Balasaheb Patare, Kalidas Apet, Kishor Dhamale, Pratibha Shinde, Rajabhau Deshmukh, Bhai S. V. Jadhav attended the meeting. Baba Adhav, Sachin Dhande, Sushila Morale, Subhash Lomte, and Subhash Kakuste worked in the Samiti in the coming days. Budhajirao Mulik, Giridhar Patil and Vijay Javandhia did not attend the meeting. Even later, they did not work with us. Many names mentioned earlier stopped active participation.

The invitations were sent to a select few, but activists from across the state were present at the meeting. We were sure some people had come just to get all the inside news and send it to Chandrakant Patil and the CM. Many had lobbied to get into the Sukanu Samiti. They had used the tactics of force and aggression to get their names on the Samiti. In future, the same people had engaged in petty politics and treason. They did not hesitate to endanger this unity while pushing personal agendas and gratifying egos. Many a time, they had targeted me. We had a glimpse of this particular quality of theirs in the third meeting of the Sukanu Samiti. As I look back, I feel sorry for how it went. I can only think of young farmers who were bearing the brunt of oppression. And one laments that these bigwigs too could not rise for the occasion.

We could but be patient. Bhai Jayant Patil and Dr Ashok Dhawale had faced this all along. But I was not used to this. All I knew was there was nothing as painful, neither my pride nor an insult, as what the farmers were facing. I was determined to bear everything and stand united in this struggle. People's power had pushed many to join hands despite having stood in opposite camps. So, it was not going to be easy to sail through.

Everyone agreed to participate in the discussion with the state government as it was happening against the backdrop of the strike and the agitations. Just after the meeting, we held a press conference at the venue. Bhai Jayant Patil welcomed all the reporters. 'The government has invited the Sukanu Samiti for discussion, and we have accepted their invitation. So, the Sukanu Samiti will take part in the meeting called by the government tomorrow on 11 June at the Sahyadri Guest House.' Bhai Jayant Patil briefed the media. Then he announced that Raju Shetty to announce the names of the delegation.

At that moment, Raghunath Patil stormed out of the press conference on hearing Raju Shetty's name. 'This is just not done!' he opposed Bhai Jayant Patil's proposition. The press conference was broadcasted live and attended by reporters from across the state. The entire state was witnessing this. The young farmers were watching all this, but the leaders were oblivious. They were just interested in keeping all the reins with them.

I shuddered.

33

11 June. The Sahyadri Guest House looked almost like a police camp. It was drizzling. We had submitted the original list of

attendees with a few minor changes. Each one was called and let in. I could not keep myself from thinking about the early morning events from the 3 June. It was a full circle, and I was standing once again at the same place. This time, the discussions were to be held in broad daylight, and the situation had changed positively for the protests. We felt a little more united.

The meeting started on time. Chandrakant Patil welcomed everyone. The news channels wanted images of the meeting, so they were called in. We had with us a charter of twenty-three demands. Ramesh Jadhav from Agrowan, a friend and an expert on agriculture, had helped us with this. I was asked to present this charter to the group of ministers. I walked up to the centre of the hall and gave the charter. Dr Ashok Dhawale, Bachchu Kadu, Justice B. G. Kolse Patil, Bhai Jayant Patil, Raju Shetty, and Raghunath Patil stood along. It showcased the unity of all farm leaders. I will never forget that moment of our unity.

The discussions began with the critical issue of loan waivers. On behalf of the group of ministers, Chandrakant Patil shared that the government was willing to waive loans of needy marginal farmers. This clearly meant that the waiver was limited only to marginal farmers and excluded those with even a little more than 5 acres of farmland. Millions of farmers from Marathwada and Vidarbha who owned more land but struggled with low produce would surely lose out. So, those who needed it the most would be kept out. Additionally, not all marginal farmers were eligible because it was offered only to the 'needy'. The conditions to determine the 'needy' were to follow.

Besides, there was no word about the loans outside crop loans, such as irrigation, construction of poly-houses, purchase of shed nets, agriculture equipment, or Emu rearing. There was no clarity on loans taken from credit co-operatives, corporations, private moneylenders, micro-finance institutions, or self-help groups (SHGs). So, we were in no position to accept this proposal. We were demanding unconditional and total loan waiver. Everybody argued strongly for this.

Chandrakant Patil wanted a resolution, come what may, fearing the impending rail roko. He asked us to wait in the hall, saying he would have a word with the Chief Minister. After some time, he called Bachchu Kadu, Bhai Jayant Patil, Raju Shetty, and Raghunath Patil. A little later, Dr Dhawale and I were called and went to the next room.

'Your demand is accepted, and the CM has agreed to the total loan waiver,' said Chandrakant Patil.

Everyone looked happy. 'Does it mean a total waiver of all loans?' I kept asking. 'A total waiver will solve all our problems, Doctor!' many of those present in the room tried to convince me.

'Let's announce this . . .!' Everyone reached the hall where the meeting with Sukanu Samiti was underway. Chandrakant Patil announced the decision of a 'total' loan waiver. 'We will only have to exclude the rich so that they do not usurp the benefits. The 2008 loan waiver benefited many such rich farmers. So to avoid this, we will have to make extra efforts. The decision on who to exclude will be made in consultation with the Sukanu Samiti. We will form a committee including a member from the Sukanu Samiti. Nobody will be excluded without your nod. We will also work upon the twenty-three demands you have presented to us. There will be a total loan waiver.' Chandrakant Patil kept repeating and emphasising that it would be a total waiver. Besides, he promised: 'New crop loans would be disbursed tomorrow, considering it is a sowing season. The time required for rolling out the loan waiver will not delay new loans.' Everybody looked happy. They felt that considering the ups and downs in the movement, we should accede to this proposal.

With everyone's nod, media was called inside the meeting hall. Chandrakant Patil informed them about the decision. Bachchu Kadu, Bhai Jayant Patil, Raju Shetty, Raghunath Patil, and I shared the decisions regarding other demands. These critical events in the farmers' struggle were being broadcasted live.

'The group of ministers on behalf of the Chief Minister has promised a total loan waiver to the farmers. They have also acceded to all our demands, including minimum support price equivalent to the cost of production plus 50 per cent. We have decided to trust the word of the Chief Minister and the group of ministers, and on that basis, we are calling off our agitation. But, if the government backtracks or cheats us to implement this, they will witness a protest of a scale unseen before. The government should take a note,' we announced our position. I thanked everyone as I was the convenor. I was happy that I could bring together people and re-organize the strike, which reached a conclusive point. We preferred to make the government accountable to its own promises rather than reject every move.

We left Sahyadri with a sense of satisfaction. Celebrations were on as we came out. Hundreds of farmers present outside were cheering, raising slogans of Zindabad. The news channels were telecasting this moment of success to all corners of the state. The news of our victory was spreading like wildfire. We were receiving calls from across the state. Young farmers were rejoicing, welcoming the announcements . . .

34

In village after village, the success of the campaign was welcomed, the leaders were felicitated. My friends cheerfully greeted me as I reached Akole. Navalevadi organized a rally and felicitated me. Friends in many big villages in the block, including Ambad, Samsherpur, and Washere, organized such events. I was not keen on such felicitations. So I used to avoid it. But Rohidas was of a different opinion. 'Doctor, if we do not go when people invite us, then, in turn, they show us their backs when we call them,' was his logic. I got his point. People gathered for these programmes and allowed us to talk to them. We could explain the position of our movements. The felicitations were followed by brainstorming on issues. New friends joined in. But all the while, in my mind, I was doubtful about the implementation of the announcements. My experience with the government was not very good. I kept fearing that they would cheat and go back on their word. The thoughts bothered me.

Meanwhile, Kalidas Apet called. He worked with Raghunath Patil. 'Doctor, we must visit the Mantralya. Sowing season is on the corner. Despite the promise, banks are not giving loans. The process of waivers is going to be lengthy. We can't wait for that. We need credit for sowing. We have to do something,' he said. He seemed to be in a hurry.

'I will organize a meeting of Sukanu Samiti and speak with everyone. We will decide whether we should go to the Mantralaya in that meeting,' I shared my opinion. Apet was not willing to wait for the meeting. 'I have already talked to Raghunath dada, and we are going there tomorrow. You also come, and we will meet the ministers,' he conveyed his decision.

I reiterated that it was not wise to decide in a hurry without consulting the Sukanu Samiti. But he was in no mood to listen. The next day, Kalidas Apet, Balasaheb Patare, and Raghunath Patil, visited the Mantralaya and met a few ministers and secretaries. I got this news from social media. And the very next day, we got an announcement about the disbursal of Rs. 10,000 as an advance loan to the farmers. We got a government order to that effect on the 14 June with some conditions so as to keep out those who did not need such assistance. The conditions were relatively rigid, and I feared that the same would be applied to the loan waiver.

All the following were termed ineligible for the advance loan: those owning a four-wheeler, farming families having a doctor, an engineer, a lawyer, a teacher, a non-teaching staff member, or a government employee including office assistants, directors of APMCs, cotton mills, dairy federations and any such cooperative, all elected representatives of Panchayat Samiti and Zilla Parishad, all those paying service tax or filing Income Tax returns, families with members having registered shops in their name. Many were excluded under a ten-point list.

I looked at these conditions as a 'test dose'. It was clear that the same would be applied to the loan waiver. Anyone with their roots in the village can understand how harmful these conditions are. Youngsters in the farming families were looking for any possible means of survival as farming was not economical. Many had taken loans to buy second-hand jeeps, pick-up vehicles, or tractors. Some had put up stalls at the roadside. Many youngsters had graduated and had engineering degrees but were sitting at home as no jobs were available. For some, reserved seats helped them enter co-operatives or panchayat structures. In the eyes of the government, all of them were now 'rich'. Their families no longer needed the advance loans. And then, why would they even require the loan waiver? This is how the total waiver was going to be tweaked.

I was disturbed by this. I immediately sent out a press note resisting these conditions and also discussed my reservations in debates on TV channels.

35

19 June 2017, 4 pm: A meeting was called at Sahyadri Guest House in Mumbai to decide the criteria for the loan waiver. An email was sent. Those in power played another game with that email. The mail mentioned that the Sukanu Samiti should send names of six people. The Samiti had thirty-five member organizations. Anyone not on the list would be unhappy, which is exactly what the government wanted. Despite our demand to accommodate more people, it did not relent on the number. They were on our backs for

the list. So, I sent a list of seven representatives of prominent unions after consulting Dr Ashok Dhawale, Raju Shetty, and Raghunath Patil. I also conveyed to these members that the final decision will be made only in the meeting of Sukanu Samiti. I knew that all the members of Sukanu were keen to participate in this meeting.

On the one hand, we were looking at some discontent among our own members, and on the other, if we did not give a list of names, the government would have happily announced that we were not ready for a discussion. This was getting trickier. It was imperative that we took everyone in confidence before this meeting.

A meeting of Sukanu Samiti was called on 19 June at the PWP office in Mumbai. We reached early morning and were welcomed by reporters who had already gathered at the venue. Once again, many people in the meeting were not in the Sukanu Samiti. I told how the government had invited only six people. As expected, this proposal was opposed as all the members were keen to join. I explained that the list was sent to avoid spreading misinformation regarding our willingness for talks. But, I reiterated that the final decision would be made here. Those who were not on the list created a ruckus, so we decided that all of us would reach Sahyadri, and a final decision will be made there.

Chandrakant Patil had played another game with the invite. The name of the committee as on the invite was: committee on criteria for waiver of unpaid loans, which meant that only those who had outstanding loans would be considered for the waiver. Even when in crisis, thousands of farmers pay off their loans in March and get new loans in April every year. All of them would become ineligible with such conditions. This was the beginning of negating the promised 'total' loan waiver.

The government had played one more game. Everybody knew that Raghunath Patil had met a few ministers after the loan waivers were announced. Now, news of Raju Shetty meeting the ministers a day before was being broadcast. Journalists and reporters asked what is the need for this meeting when two prominent leaders had already met the ministers.

Chandrakant Patil was clever with his moves. He announced a total loan waiver to take out the steam of our agitations. Then, he got some of us on his side and played the advance loan card. He used that opportunity to bring in the criteria for exclusion, which would be applied to the loan waiver. The stage was set. And by calling it a committee on criteria for waiver of *unpaid* loans, farmers who repaid the loans on time were kept out. An invitation to six members was a conscious move to create unrest within the Sukanu Samiti. And the news about meetings with these two leaders cast doubt on the entire process. Chandrakant Patil had done all his homework well and was making planned moves. The fight was getting harder and harder.

All of us in the Sukanu Samiti started towards the Sahyadri Guest House. The news channels played just this one news: Meeting of Sukanu Samiti. All the events were telecast live. We were in a fight with the government. Though I was their prime enemy for many amongst us, and I was held responsible for excluding names from the delegation. I was reeling under this pressure as we approached Sahyadri.

36

As we reached Sahyadri, Chandrakant Patil and many other ministers were already there. Seeing our delegation of forty to forty-five people, he played his trump card, 'Give us a list of six, at the most seven names. Nobody else will be let in.' His voice was way too shrill. His persona was nothing compared to the one requesting us to stop the agitation promising a total loan waiver. This led to a hullabaloo, and many attacked me, asking why they were invited if they couldn't be part of the delegation. The ploy to divide us was working. Chandrakant Patil announced that six or seven members should join them in the next room, and he left the room along with Girish Mahajan. I was trying to calm down our people without anyone else for support. Dr Dhawale was not present as he was in Kerala. Raju Shetty got up and silently went to the next room. Raghunath Patil followed him. I tried to talk through, convincing everyone that the final decision would be taken only with their consent. But nobody was in a mood to listen. Finally, after repeated calls from the discussion room, I went there, gathering all the documents and my diary. Bachchu Kadu, Bhai Jayant Patil, Raghunath Patil, Raju Desale, Raju Shetty, Sanjay Ghatnekar, and I were present for the discussion. Chandrakant Patil and a few other ministers and officers represented the government.

And, he pulled out yet another card. He started reading out the criteria for the advance loan of Rs. 10,000 from the government order. As he proceeded, I took an objection. 'These criteria are for advance credit of Rs. 10,000. We have gathered for deciding the criteria for the loan waiver. So let us discuss that,' I said as politely as I could. Patil chose to ignore me and went on. The moment he asked if we needed to 'ease certain conditions', some leaders started suggesting changes. My doubts had come true. We were in for yet another deceit – a re-run of the events from 3 June.

The loan waiver criteria were based on those for the crop credit of Rs. 10,000. Suggestions were coming in even from farmers in the meeting. Patil was really good with his homework. Incensed by the entire discussion, I stood up and said, 'On the backdrop of the farmers' strike, you had announced a total loan waiver. At that time, you made no distinction between paid and unpaid loans. You had mentioned a few criteria to keep the 'rich' out from the benefits. But now, you have come up with this list. This is not right.' Patil looked at me, paused for a while, and resumed his discussions with the leaders. The picture was clear, and I was being sidelined again.

Members of the delegation kept suggesting changes. I simply had no role there. And Chandrakant Patil threw another bombshell. 'The government has looked at all your suggestions positively. And thus, we are ready for a complete waiver, with some changes to the criteria, of unpaid loans up to Rs. 1 lakh.' Patil told us as if declaring a decision.

'What do you mean by "up to 1 lakh"?' I objected loudly. 'Dada, you had promised a total loan waiver. What is this limit of Rs. 1 lakh?'

There was an eerie silence. I was waiting for a few more voices of protest. But nobody uttered a word. Chandrakant Patil was fiddling with some papers, a mischievous smile on his face. I was furious. I stood up one more time and asked him, 'Dada, what are you up to? What is this limit of Rs. 1 lakh? And that too with pre-conditions? What is all this?' I was fuming.

'Doctor, have some patience. This is just right,' Patil murmured. He was pretty confident of his preparations.

I sat down feeling hopeless. Raju Desale and Sanjay Ghatnekar sat next to me. 'We are being duped. People will not forgive us. Our fight is for a total loan waiver. And look at this limit of Rs. 1 lakh and all these rigid criteria. At no cost, we should agree to this,' I told Raju Desale. Bachchu Kadu looked at me sympathetically. He possibly agreed with me. I decided to intervene one more time. 'Dada, thank you for your proposal of [a waiver upto] Rs. 1 lakh. Other members of the Sukanu Samiti are waiting in the hall. Let us present this proposal to them, and after their consent, we will go ahead,' I told Patil.

'Doctor, why discuss any more? You have won big. Go back to your villages and rejoice,' Patil said with his signature impish smile.

There was no point being there in that room. I signalled to Desale and Ghatnekar. They nodded. We immediately got up and went to the hall where other members of the Sukanu Samiti were waiting. Raghunath Patil and Bachchcu Kadu followed, and so did Raju Shetty.

There was pin-drop silence in the hall. The mood was remarkably different from before the meeting. Everyone looked serious and in the mood to listen. Bhai Jayant Patil summarised the entire discussion. Raghunath Patil added a few points. I kept quiet, and I did feel a little hopeless. I went up to Bachchu Kadu, and in a very soft voice, I shared my opinion about this entire episode. 'Trust me . . . If we accept the limit of Rs. 1 lakh for the waiver with all these criteria, people will never forgive us. The government is trying to use us for their motives. My intuition will never go wrong. Let us oppose these preconditions . . .' I kept repeating my views.

As he listened to me, he leaned back on this chair and asked in his peculiar style, 'What do we do then?'

'Let's burn the copies of government order regarding advance crop loan of Rs. 10,000 and protest these moves. Let the message be unequivocal that we are not for any such loan waiver within a limit of Rs. 1 lakh and with such rigid preconditions,' I said.

With his famous smile, he replied, 'Why outside? Why not burn it here, right now?'

This was a clear signal of his support. I was relieved. I returned to my chair.

As Raghunath Patil finished his speech, Karan Gaykar appealed to speak. 'Doctor, please share your views,' members from Nashik were pestering me to talk.

Before the meeting, these same people were unhappy with me, blaming me for not including them in the delegation. But now, their request was genuine. I was a little surprised but also quite relieved. So, I stood up and shared my views very briefly but as effectively as possible. I focussed on the dangers of this 'limit of Rs. 1 lakh, that too only for unpaid loans or defaulters and how it was unfair for those repaying their debts on time. I also underlined how nothing outside crop loans was included in the waiver, and that negates the promise of a total loan waiver.' I sincerely stated my opinion, 'We should never accept this loan waiver proposal for unpaid loans below Rs. 1 lakh. Instead, we should protest by burning the copies of the government order regarding the advance loan of Rs. 10,000.'

I think it hit where it was supposed to hit. Many stood up in my support. Most of the members seemed to agree with me, which led to a clamour in the hall. Surprised, I asked Desale how did it change? He smiled and said, 'When you were not allowed to talk, I sent out a message saying, 'The discussion is headed the wrong way, Doctor is being pressurised. The effect is for you to see.' I was impressed with his smartness which, along with my presentation, had veered these people to our side.

Chandrakant Patil was still playing smart. It seemed that he simply didn't care to wait for our decision. I do not know why, but he was absolutely sure that the Sukanu Samiti was ready to accept his proposal. Maybe it was his background work that made him believe that. He called the reporters inside the room.

'We had a positive discussion with the Sukanu Samiti. The government has proposed completely waiving off unpaid loans below Rs. 1 lakh. We are coming to an agreement,' he informed the reporters.

The news channels telecast the press conference live. Soon, the news channels started flashing 'Loan waiver limited to Rs. 1 lakh, with preconditions and criteria . . .!' . Many of us began to get those screenshots on our phones. People were puzzled. 'What kind of loan waiver is this?' Phone calls of angry protestors soon followed. Reactions started coming in even before we had reached a consensus. And members lost their patience. Some stormed out shouting, 'Doctor was right. Come, let's burn that government resolution. Waving the copies of the government resolution, they angrily came out, not waiting for the farm leaders even to get up from their chairs. Sukanu Samiti was protesting the decision, raising slogans against it. There was a big commotion in Sahyadri.

Hearing the slogans, reporters covering Chandrakant Patil's press conference ran out of the room. Sukanu Samiti members had reached the outside gate till then. Raju Shetty and others were following. On that night, slogans reached a high pitch: Down with the BJP government! *Phadnavis Sarkar Murdabad! Shetkari Ekjut Zindabad!* (Down with Fadnavis' Government! Long live the unity of farmers)!' The sound of the slogans filled the air. Everyone left Patil's press conference. Once again, the news channels caught farmers' voices on their cameras and shared them across the state. Now, Raju Shetty and Raghunath Patil were at the forefront of burning the government resolution and saying how the government tried cheating the farmers. Bachchu Kadu, Khandubaba, Rohidas, and I, were standing in one corner watching the charade. We had outdone Chandrakant Patil, the bully. Once again, the young farmers came out winners. We had won the lost battle. The flame had turned into fire. The road towards Sahyadri was illuminating in its glow.

III

37

Sukanu Samiti opposed the deceitful announcement of loan waiver with set conditions and criteria because, in the meeting with the group of ministers, it was announced that the number of unpaid loans and landholding size would not affect the waiver. We had stopped our agitation only because we were promised this. But now, by including only defaulters, all those who repaid their loans regularly were being excluded from the scheme.

It is common for farmers to borrow money to repay the loans by the end of March and then get a new loan to pay back the borrowed amount. That does not mean that agriculture is profitable, and so they are able to repay. They are equally in crisis. But technically, they are not defaulters. So, it was unfair to apply the waiver to defaulters alone.

Against the backdrop of drought and farmers' suicides, the government repeatedly restructured their loans. So, although in crisis, they do not appear on the list of defaulters. It was not fair to deny them the benefits of the waiver.

Many banks had directly restructured these loans without even consulting the farmers. The loans were restructured into medium-term loans. Technically, even these farmers were no longer defaulters. Many farmers had put all their cash in denotified currency notes into their saving accounts during demonetisation. Again, the banks had diverted this money to their loan accounts and restructured their loans without their consent. All such farmers were excluded from the waiver under these new criteria.

The government had declared that only those who were

defaulters as of 30 June 2016 were eligible for the advance loan of Rs. 10,000. The same deadline was to be applied for loan waiver, and all those borrowers in the coming year, till 30 June 2017, were kept out.

Farmers had also borrowed money for various other things: poultry, Emu rearing, constructing poly-houses, shade nets, for land levelling, or buying agri-equipments and tools. Due to the deliberate reduction of prices of agricultural produce coupled with losses suffered due to natural disasters, the farmers were unable to repay these loans. But the loan waiver was not extended to these farmers and those who had borrowed from private moneylenders, micro-finance institutions and gold loan schemes.

On top of all this, there was a limit of Rs. 1 lakh for the waiver. If the farmers pay off their loans over and above Rs. 1 lakh, they are eligible for the waiver. This was not a loan 'waiver' but rather a ploy for 'recovery'. There was some vague announcement of some benefit for those with regular repayments. The word 'total' had lost all its meaning. So, we could but protest as there was no other way. We had to restart our protests.

38

Sukanu Samiti took decided to reject all efforts by the government to limit the benefit of the loan waiver. And for this reason, farmers had more faith in us now. We feared that the government would try and bypass the discussions with the Sukanu Samiti, and that is precisely what Chandrakant Patil did. He started meeting members of various political parties. He wanted to take charge, minimize our importance, and make decisions convenient to him.

So, he first met Uddhav Thakare. Then, along with CM Fadnavis, he went and met Sharad Pawar. He spoke with the media after this visit, where he announced that he was trying to get everyone to agree to the loan waiver. He declared that he would soon meet Radhakrishna Vikhe Patil and Ashok Chavan. And, he did not forget to tell the reporters that he had already discussed this with Raju Shetty.

The very next day, on 24 June 2017, CM Fadnavis called a press conference and announced a loan waiver without consulting the Sukanu Samiti. The waiver was up to Rs. 1.5 lakh and with certain terms and conditions. Bowing to our staunch protest, the earlier limit of one lakh was increased by fifty thousand, and some norms were relaxed. But most of the norms continued, resulting in keeping lakhs of farmers outside the ambit of this waiver. On the contrary, the CM claimed that this was the biggest and almost a historical loan waiver in this country. He claimed that eighty-nine lakh farmers would benefit from this, and forty lakh farmers would be cleared of all dues from their *saat baara*[4]. The limit of one and a half lakh meant that all those who had more debt had to clear the remaining amount in one instalment; then only would they be eligible for this waiver. All those who paid off their debts on time did not get much apart from the Rs.15,000-25,000 incentives.

We called for a meeting the next day to discuss and take a stand on this announcement. Dr Dhawale, Bhai Jayant Patil, Raghunath Dada, Sanjay Ghatanekar and many other members were present in this meeting held at CPI office, Janashakti at Worli. Bachchu Kadu called and supported Sukanu Samiti's stand. Raju Shetty did not come.

Sukanu Samiti declared that this loan waiver was all but bluff. A decision to launch a statewide agitation was made. All key office bearers of the Kisan Sabha were invited to the meeting. Their collective strength would help widen our outreach and the campaign.

We announced the statewide campaign at the press conference, which was very well attended by reporters. The campaign would

---

[4] *Saat baara*: *saat* (seven) and *baara* (twelve) are two records of land entitlement which hold information on ownership of land, crops, debt, liability, and so on.

start from Nashik and culminate in Pune. Massive rallies and Shetkari Elgar Parishad would be organized in 14 key sites.

39

We were trying to bring all the farmer unions from Maharashtra on one platform of the Sukanu Samiti. There were similar efforts at the national level where more than 200 organizations were coming together as Akhil Bharatiya Kisan Sangharsh Samanvay Samiti (All India Kisan Sangharsh Co-ordination Committee – AIKSCC). Rallies were planned across various states to raise awareness and unite the farmers. Hannan Mollah – the National General Secretary of AIKS, Raju Shetty, V. M. Singh, and Yogendra Yadav took the lead. The rally would pay tribute to the protesting farmers killed by police in Mandsaur in Madhya Pradesh.

The rally was going to enter Maharashtra on 9 July, and many events to welcome it were planned across the Nashik district on 10 July. Raju Shetty had decided to be present for these programmes. Sukanu Samiti rallies too were scheduled for 9 July. Having two separate rallies to unite farmers, planned on the same day, was not a good idea. If both the rallies come together in Nashik, it will indeed send a message of unity among the farmers. But the differences among the leaders had made any such coordination difficult.

But I kept at it, trying to coordinate between all the leaders. I had hardly thought that this same effort would bite me in future. I was sincerely trying to get two important leaders on one stage. It almost seemed childish. After much effort, we postponed Sukanu Samiti's event by a day, and now the national rally and the state campaign were to start on the 10 July from Nashik from the same platform.

Activists from Nashik were very keen that the Sukanu Samiti starts its campaign from their district. Considering their unwavering support during the strike when everything was falling apart, it was difficult to ignore their wish. We felt that the Nashik team would prepare everything well, like the last two gatherings. But we were in for a surprise. Everybody thought that people would attend in large numbers, and no one took much effort. Not many people came to the event. And the first-ever rally in the state has a lukewarm response. I was sad.

Around 200-300 activists took part in the national event. Another two-three hundred came for the Sukanu event. Altogether, not more than six hundred people were present. A month back, we had a resounding response to our programme here, at the same venue. But, today, unfettered, our farm leaders were happy gratifying their ego. They chose to display the internal split right on the stage. In Maharashtra, the all India yatra was represented by Raju Shetty, and a person invited by him was delivering his speech. Raghunath Patil's supporters stated sloganeering and insulted the speaker. Once again, they proved that the ego of their leaders is far bigger than the farmers' movement or the unity of farmers' unions. This spoilt the mood of the programme. The media was witness to this. I could see the Sukanu Samiti's future. It troubled me. But I had to keep going.

We had failed at the inaugural event. But we had no option but to make the upcoming thirteen meetings a grand success. It was clear that Kisan Sabha had to participate for the events to be successful. Dr Ashok Dhawale and Kisan Gujar had promised to be with us in the entire programme. To have Dr Dhawale with us for all fourteen days was great, and we were a bit relieved.

The Nashik rally was a fiasco. That same night, we sat together late in the evening and called up all our Kisan Sabha leaders. We explained how important it was for these rallies to receive a good response. I pleaded with them to prepare well. After doing all this homework, I lay down. The very next day, we started our two-week-long yatra on a specially decorated 'rath'. This was the fourth such statewide campaign in the last three years.

The second rally was at Vikramgad in the Palghar district. Vishwanath Patil of Kunbi Sena had mobilised along with Kisan Sabha. Thane-Palghar is Kisan Sabha forte. Godavari and Shamrao Parulekar mobilized the Warli Adivasis for the historical fight [against the landlords and British], and Lal Bavta found its roots here. The mantle was carried forward by the able leadership of Krushna Khopkar, L. B. Dhangar, former MP Lahanu Kom, and many Adivasi leaders. And now, it is for Dr Ashok Dhawale, Barkya Mangat, Mariam Dhawale, Ratan Budhar and many prominent leaders that the movement is still going strong.

Dr Ashok Dhawale has been fighting for the rights of oppressed workers from Thane and Palghar since 1978, when he was an office-bearer of the SFI. He comes from a well-off family. His father was a well-known doctor, and Dr Dhawale could have lived a very comfortable life. As a student of the Nair Hospital, Mumbai, he came face-to-face with the harsh realities of the poor, living in 10-by-10 dingy rooms of the slums in front of his college. It was inhuman. Moved by their condition, he rejected comfort and actively participated in the workers' movement. In 1978, he joined the Communist Party of India (Marxist). In the students' movement, he took the state-level responsibility in the SFI, DYFI, and later Kisan Sabha. He went on to become the National President of the AIKS.

One is simply astonished by his journey of the last forty-one. He has fulfilled every responsibility with the same vigour. One such instance was the national convention of farmers organized by the Kisan Sabha in 2006 in Nashik. It was a historic movement, and more than one lakh farmers attended the convention. Dr Dhawale, the then MLA Jiva Pandu Gavit and their comrades made this possible. The AIKS owes a great deal to Dr Dhawale for its current position in the movement and the scope of its work on many fronts. Personally, it was Dr Dhawale who brought me into the folds of Kisan Sabha. I was with the SFI till then. And he did not stop there. He made all efforts to ensure I stayed. He was there to boost me whenever I felt low, demoralized, or depressed. And it is not just me. Many amongst us owe a lot to Dr Dhawale.

Since 2017, Dr Dhawale has been the national president of the AIKS and a member of the Central Committee of CPI (M). His work is now pan-India. He is in Kerala, sometime in Bengal, Assam, or Tamil Nadu. He is constantly on the go for the AIKS activities. But he is still quite involved in Maharashtra and has a keen interest in youth, workers', and farmers' movements. He is still abreast with the daily activities of the Thane-Palghar unit of the AIKS.

Comrade Mariam is his life partner. She is strong and resolute. She started her work through the students' movement in 1979 and was later active in the women's movement. Since 1994, she has been looking after the activities of the All-India Democratic Women's Association (AIDWA) in Thane and Palghar. Her journey is filled with many ups and downs, many bitter-sweet memories, and struggles. Mariam did not stop. She overcame it all. Now, she is the general secretary of the AIDWA, and she looks after the network across the country. Still, she keeps an eye on all that happens in Thane and Palghar. Both Mariam and Dr Dhawale have devoted their entire lives to the workers' movement. Today's meeting of the Sukanu Samiti was a result of their commitment and contribution.

The AIKS had put all its strength to make the Vikramgadh rally a grand success. A minimum of seven to eight thousand farmers arrived. Women farmers were significant in their numbers. Vishwanath Patil had mobilized the Kunbi Sena network. The response was tremendous. Though we had booked a big hall, the venue was packed. Slogans and speeches reverberated in the hall. We succeeded in undoing the failure of yesterday's event. It was a big relief. Comrade Ashok Dhawale, Barkya Mangat, comrade Mariam Dhawale, and Ratan Budhar – hats off to all of them.

Namdev Gavade from Kisan Sabha affiliated to CPI had participated in the rally. The next day, we had a rally in Kalwan. Gavade wanted to organize a few meetings in Bhivandi-Kalyan before heading to Kalwan. We wanted to reach Nashik after the programme. The next day we were to reach Kalwan. But we could not refuse him. Farmers here were protesting against the proposed land acquisition for an upcoming airport. There had been some scuffle with the police. Some of the activists were behind bars. And villages were terrified. Gavade felt that our presence would boost the morale of the villagers. Heeding people's demands, we decided to go. Many CPI activists welcomed us on the way. Khandubaba, Namdev Gavade, Sushila Morale, and I went to the venue. It was evening by the time we reached. There was a strong police presence. Many young farmers were arrested. The situation was tense. The entire village had gathered at the temple. Local activists had arranged everything quite well. We spoke after the local leaders. We tried to build the confidence of the villagers, and we left. We reached Nashik at 1.30 am.

Jeeva Pandu Gavit had put all his might into making the Kalwan rally a grand success. The hall was filled with farmers. Raghunath Patil and Bachchu Kadu were not present for the events in Thane-Palghar and Kalwan. Raju Shetty was in Gujarat for the Kisan rally. We were mobilizing and organizing all these events.

Many onion farmers from the vicinity attended the Kalwan rally. They were worried as onion prices kept falling. India is one of the leading producers of onion worldwide. There are three seasons – Rabi, Kharif, and late Kharif. India produces around 18.9 million metric tonnes of onions every year. Maharashtra, Karnataka, Madhya Pradesh, Gujarat and Bihar are the onion producing states in the country. Maharashtra alone produces 40 per cent of the total output. There is an international demand for the Indian onion due to its taste, size and, most importantly, its flesh. We export around

1.2 million metric tonnes of onion after fulfilling the domestic demand.

In India, onion is available almost all through the year. The Kharif onion reaching the markets during October to December is just 20 per cent of the entire produce. Another 20 per cent arrives from January to March. This is cultivated in late Kharif. The Rabi produce is harvested from April onwards to June. This is almost 60 per cent of all produce, and this is stored and sold till October or November. Thus, markets have onion almost all through the year.

We fulfil the domestic demand and then export. We have a year-round supply. So, ideally, the prices should be steady. But that is not to be the case. Onion prices are extremely volatile. The entire nation feels the heat. And this volatility is a ground for politics. Hoarders, traders, and exporters exploit the farmers' woes every season. Onion is bought at a pittance and hoarded. Supplies dry up, and consumers shell out extra money. Both the farmers and consumers are set to lose.

The government is surprisingly quite sensitive when it comes to onion pricing. It is extremely cautious when consumers complain about onion prices. The same consumers can become a nuisance in times of elections. So, it starts importing and curbs exports. Prices are brought down, which has a debilitating impact on farmers. Onion is on the list of essential commodities, making it easy for the government to intervene.

According to The Essential Commodities Act (ECA), the state has the right to intervene in the market to regulate prices. And it also has the responsibility that the farmers get a fair price for their produce. The state asserts its right but completely forgets its responsibility.

The onion question is not a difficult one to solve. It needs a just and fair state that judiciously implements the laws. The farmers have time and again demanded a fair price for their onions. They want a regulation against hoarding. Their demands included warehouses, credit, aid to set up onion processing units, efforts to reduce the production cost, development of infrastructure and just policies for import and export. The farmers at this gathering were telling but the truth.

42

A public meeting was organized at Sangamner on 13 July. Ahmednagar being my district, the programme had to be a grand success. The media was watching. Abhijit Dighe, Anil Dethe, Kiran Khairnar and Shantaram Haase of Bhumiputra Shetkari Sanghatana, Mahesh Navale from Akole, Nilesh Talekar, Rohida Dhumal, Dr Sandip Kadlag, and Santodh Wadekar had worked very hard for the event. Bachchu Kadu had agreed to grace the occasion. He along with Ganesh Jagtap, Sanjay Ghatanekar, and Vitthal Pawar, were the main speakers. We had a good response from the farmers. The hall was packed.

Implementation of recommendations by the Swaminathan Commission was vital to overcoming the agrarian crisis. This demand was now quite popular, thanks to the farmers' movement. But many were still not aware of the exact recommendations that this commission made for the national farmers' policy. So we had translated these and published them in a small booklet. Dr Uday Narkar of the Kisan Sabha had translated the content, and the booklet was available for farmers at rallies. We distributed many at the Sangamner event, which gave us a fillip.

On 14 July, Kishor Dhamale had organized a rally in Sakri in Dhule district. We travelled overnight and reached Sakri early in the morning. There was a big crowd of farmers. Raghunath Patil was present for this one and all the programmes that followed.

Some farm leaders who had worked with the late Sharad Joshi came and met us. They shared many events from their days with him. Listening to those memories gave us goosebumps. Our discussion steered to the exploitation of farmers in the APMCs and farmers shared their agony.

The very structures that were meant to protect the farmers were looting them. The auction had almost turned into a slaughter. It was distressing to hear how farmers suffered. Inside the APMC, a select few traders are given licenses to purchase the farm produce, assuming that the licensed traders will abide by the law, will not dupe the farmers and offer a fair price for their produce. In reality, many traders, exporters of those engaged in food processing who are willing to offer better prices, cannot participate in the auctions as they do not hold a license. The license raj does not allow for healthy competition, and it becomes a weapon to monopolize the market. These licensed traders gang up, and prices fall. Produce grown on farmers' sweat, and blood is offered a pittance. Farmers are in a trap. They have to repay debts incurred on production and transport. Lack of storage facilities leaves them with no option but to accept the unfair offers. The auctioneering is just a façade. The traders fix the price beforehand. The farmer is looted. But this is not the only loot. At every pre- and post-harvesting step, the helpless farmer, who has no other option, is looted.

The traders purchase the produce but do not immediately pay the farmers. Here the *arthiya* works as an agent between the farmer and the trader. But his services are not for free. They charge 3 to 6 per cent as their commission, which is called *adat*. Farmers pay up to Rs. 4000 crores as *adat* every year.

Farmers have been voicing various demands regarding this unfair system. The auctions need to be transparent, exploitative practices such as *kaatla* and *judi* should be banned, electronic weighing scales to prevent cheating, cash transactions by traders which will end the unfair system of *adat* are some of the changes that farmers demand. They also want in place protective measures such as using farm produce as collateral for loans, cold storage, basic infrastructure in place, a fair and just competition that is not restricted by the 'license raj' and strict implementation of the policy for MSP that includes perishable goods to name a few.

The demands are not new. They have been voiced for years – generation after generation.

The government is happy to create illusions of online markets or e-markets as reforms. It does not address the actual situation and is detrimental to farmers. All those who had gathered at Sakri were crying their heart out. Their sorrow and their hope disturbed me.

43

A public meeting was planned at Chandur Baazar in the Amravati district. Bachchu Kadu represents this constituency; thus, he had put in a lot of effort to make this meeting a success. Mahadev Garpawar and other Kisan Sabha activists had mobilized a sizable number of farmers. We reached the venue in a rally, on a truck decorated specially for that. We could see that Kadu had a personal connection with people.

Bachchu bhau (brother) is a gem of a person. There are no two ways with him. If he decides something, then there is no turning back. Many fraudulent officials have faced his ire which is followed by litigation leading to debates and accolades resulting in more support for his actions. Once, he thrashed some officials from Mantralaya. One can argue whether this is right or wrong, but Bachchu bhau stands firmly behind the poor, old and infirm. He never fails to support deserted and widowed women. He appears pretty aggressive, but he is a kind person at heart, surrounded by his activists. He is a fine man who stands out in the political circle. His presence in the Sukanu rally would certainly cheer up the mood. And his speech – his pointed critique with taunts and satire would unfailingly bring cheers and laughs – his threats and challenges received applause. We had organized our first public conference in Nashik under the aegis of the Sukanu Samiti after it was formed on 8 June. It was the first event after successfully foiling all divisive attempts to end the farmers' strike. The venue was beaming with people. And Bachchu bhau stood up for his speech. He declared that we would protest at Varsha, the chief minister's residence. But he didn't stop there. He announced that we would bomb the place! That was it. People clapped and cheered and burst into laughter. The headlines of the newspapers carried just this single headline – 'Plan to bomb the Chief Minister's residence'!

Everyone knew that he was not a man who believed in violent means. It is his style of speech, and he says all such things. He never fails to mention Chhatrapati Shivaji in his speeches. In his unique style, he will stress that Chhatrapati did not belong to a single caste or a religion. He was the king of the labourers. He would often end his speech with a warning:

'You might have seen radical action based on caste and religion. But you are yet to witness what happens when young farmers take that radical path.

We will see when young farmers mobilize and take up radical action.

It is going to cost you dearly.

We will see.'

Slightly tilting his neck on one side, in a signature Bachchu bhau style, he speaks in a typical dialect from Vidarbha, which often receives cheers from the crowd, sloganeering, screams and whistles.

I was impressed by another aspect of his work, his support network for patients and their relatives who might require blood or surgery, those who need to travel to Pune-Mumbai for better treatment, or those seeking monetary aid from the PM or CM relief fund. Bachchu bhau was their answer. His activists listen to these needs and find solutions.

Well done!

He had organized a blood donation camp before starting the Sukanu meeting. Ten to fifteen cots were placed for the donors who stood in long lines. This was commendable work, something that one should follow. I started thinking about how I could replicate this in Akole. I must.

44

From Chandur Bazaar, we went to Khamgaon in the Buldhana district. There, too we had a good rally. Kisan Sabha activists Anil Gaikwad, Dada Raypure, and Jitendra Chopde had put in a great effort, and it paid off. We felt encouraged by the increasing response to our meetings. Many cultivating cotton and soybean had come for the rally, and they complained that they were not getting any benefits under the crop insurance schemes even when incurring losses.

We saw that farmers were trapped. On the one hand, it was the state policies, and on the other, it was the natural calamities such as drought, hailstorms, cyclones, floods, landslides, dry spells, pest infestations, and newer diseases. The new crop insurance schemes were meant to protect farmers in such situations. But it turned out to be more beneficial to the insurance companies than the farmers. This had angered them, and they demanded that the lacunae be removed.

What were these demands raised by farmers in various public programmes?

These demands are: A comprehensive cover for all crops and not against select crops in select circles. Precise definitions of drought, flood, and hailstorm to ensure that insurance companies do not avoid settling the claims. A provision for 100 per cent payment in the circumstances of crop failure and no sowing. Full amount to be paid when natural disasters such as floods, landslides, hailstorms, and excessive rainfall damage crops, soil, and farm structures such as bunding. To set up an independent, impartial, and fair agency to handle cases of non-settlement of claims and objections. To set up modern weather forecast centres in each circle which will help evaluate damages and weather forecasts to be displayed on government websites to bring in transparency. Use of advanced technology and methodology for cultivation and measurement of damages. To end corrupt practices in the system of crop cutting and insurance cover for damages during storage and transport of the produce.

On 17 July, we had organized a programme in Wardha. Janrao Nagmote, Yashvant Zade, and activists from Prahar had worked hard for this. There was a motorbike rally ahead of the main event in the evening. People had come from faraway places. The programme was well-received.

We went to the Sevagram Ashram after our programme was over. It was calm and soothing. I remember we had once planned a 'Jail Bharo' in Ahmednagar on the issue of the right to the forest lands. Five to six thousand people were to take out a rally in our support. 'Jail Bharo' usually means a token arrest and immediate release. A technical entry on paper mostly. Just an act. Police knew only this. But we were determined to go to jail.

If they arrested a thousand people or more, they had to put us in different central jails as no single jail had that capacity. So were shifted to the Aurangabad, Kolhapur, Nashik, and Yerawada central jails. I was in Kolhapur Central Jail along with a hundred activists. During my stay there, I had read all the available books on Gandhiji. That helped me change many of my positions and perception. It transformed from within. I learnt these things afresh: satyagraha, non-violence, peace, self-reliance, and penance. And this had an impact on our agitations and many decisions. It still has.

And, now, I was here in Sevagram, visiting Bapu Kuti. All the memories from that time in the jail came back to me. And so did all the readings.

Wonderful!

Our next stop was Kinwat town in Nanded district on 18 July. Due to the prolonged dry spell, farmers were faced with the second sowing in the Kharif. We could read that stress on their faces. They had spent a lot of money on the first sowing, and crops were wilting due to the dry spell. Now, there was no option but to borrow and sow the seeds again. But where could they get the loan as they already had dues, causing tremendous stress. They were letting their hearts out and telling us that they would have sowed a little late if they knew the accurate weather forecasts.

This is how farming became unviable for our farmers. The support provided by the state for this unviable venture was equally unreliable. The weather forecasts provided by the state were not to be believed at all. Farmers were compelled to sow again. There is a desperate need for timely and accurate forecasts on rain and natural disasters along the lines of the systems in developed countries. We have to bring in improved systems in this field using Ground Weather Radar and a network of sensors. Looking at those farmers and the pain on their faces reminded us of this need.

Arjun Ade from Kisan Sabha, farm leader Shankar Sidam and Kishor Pawar led the programme in Kinwat. Farmers had come in large numbers, and many demanded that ownership of the lands belonging to the temple trusts be given to the tillers. Farmers were agitating for this cause.

46

The next meeting was in Parbhani on 19 July. The public gathering saw a massive response, with more than ten thousand farmers attending it. Deepak Lipane, Rameshwar Paul, Ramkrushna Shere, Uddhav Paul, Vilas Babar from Kisan Sabha, and other activists from farmers' unions mobilized the farmers. They had been protesting for many years around the water crisis in

Marathwada. Their work had focused on permanent solutions for irrigation. Therefore, the meeting addressed irrigation and water issues along with freedom from debt and the MSP.

From here, we headed to Dharur in the Beed district. Along the roads, we witnessed how the canal network was in shambles. Water from the Jayakwadi dam is released through these canals. It was disastrous.

We saw how fields had dried out due to a lack of water.

And people – battered and burnt by the crisis.

'The roots of poverty in our country lie in the rainfed farming.' I could not get my mind off this statement by Sharad Joshi.

Maharashtra Water and Irrigation Commission had presented its report in 1999, wherein it was estimated that with the available surface water, we could increase our irrigation capacity to 8.5 million hectares of farmland. But, even after spending huge amounts of money, we could only reach 4.73 million hectares as our irrigation capacity. And what pains us the most is that the actual irrigation did not even cross 29.5 million hectares out of this capacity. This means that focused efforts would have led to irrigating 3.76 million hectares more. Not to forget that these estimates are from 1995. The progress in science and technology should, in fact, help us irrigate double this area. We could have won our battle with the persistent drought, once and for all. But nothing happened on the ground.

Why is this disparity in the capacity to irrigate and actual irrigation? One reason specific to Maharashtra is the prevalent method of unrestricted irrigation. The old and dilapidated canal distribution system results in almost 70 per cent loss through vapourization and percolation. The sight of such old, damaged canals on our way reminded us of the need for an efficient pipe distribution network.

The issue of water scarcity is not about the non-availability of water. Compared with other areas, Maharashtra receives good rainfall. The real problem is 'unequal' distribution and 'unreasonable' use. The western coast of Konkan gets an annual rainfall of 3,500 mm, whereas the rain shadow areas on the east of Sahyadris hardly get 450 mm. The disparity has its roots in nature, but it is cruel!

Considering this disparity in rainfall and the specific geographical situation of the state, it is improper that irrigation and water availability policies were determined regionally and not according to the river basin. The state's Water Resources Department (WRD) also works in this framework. We need to understand that the regional disputes around water are distressing and unscientific.

The solution to these disputes is ensuring that all the rightful water users from head to tail in the river basin get their entitled water quota. A just and scientific framework for a water plan in a river basin will lead the way. The piped distribution network will also cut down losses, and all the users will get their entitled quota through equitable water distribution.

The state took a step in this direction, framing a new water policy that decided to measure and distribute water to all water users. Management, operation, and monitoring of water resources through the participation of people was the guiding principle, and to achieve that – water user associations were formed. Though the state followed the principle of equitable water distribution, it was not possible to implement it through the same old systems. A piped distribution network was essential.

There is complete anarchy when it comes to water. There are laws in place and rules but flaws that make it easy for the rich and powerful to tweak it their way. Water thefts through breaches of canals and private submersible pumps are widespread. Industries have been pardoned for water thefts. All this happens in a social milieu where 'water lords' rule. There is a need to put an end to this anarchy. Strong and undeterred will and faith in justice and the modern piped distribution technology will pave the way.

For the last four years, the state has been implementing a

scheme called – *maagel tyala shet tale* (farm pond on demand). The basic idea is that a farmer will be able to utilize the rainwater by collecting it in a farm pond. But, on the ground, people were indiscriminately extracting age-old groundwater stores using bore wells and storing it in open tanks to vapourize. Farm ponds were turning into water vapourizing machines, and the state was distributing these machines on demand. But there were no serious efforts to recharge the groundwater.

The drought continued. The farmers' woes are never-ending. Lack of political will, inadequate finances, corruption, politicking, and the use of muscle power continue to plague the water sector. The regional dispute around water and criminal attempts to divide and put the farmers against one another is a ploy to cover up their failures. We have not been able to move ahead. It is not going to help in future. The dilapidated canal systems, wastage of water, and parched farmlands of Marathwada were ringing a warning bell. Pained and distressed, we headed towards Dharur.

47

The flaws in the implementation of the loan waiver scheme were now coming to the fore. The state had asked for online applications from farmers to make the process transparent. But it was a big headache for the farmers who had to spend days standing in the queue to submit their forms. This charade continued for the next five months and all in the name of transparency. The deadline was extended many times. There were discrepancies in the information furnished by the farmers, submitted by the banks, and on the Aadhar cards. The historical waiver announced by the CM was a historical menace for farmers. Farmers could not get new loans because of the blunder in numbers, announcements, pre-conditions, and online processes. The long list of preconditions was enough to disillusion the farmers. We were putting these facts out in our rallies and speeches and were appealing to everyone to gear up for a bigger fight.

The programme at Dharur on 20 July saw huge crowds. Mohan Lamb and Uttam Mane of Kisan Sabha, Kalidas Apet from Shetkari Sanghatana, and Sushila Morale from the Sangharsh Samiti had put in a lot of work. Datta Dake from the Shetmajoor Union chaired the event. While he shared the problems faced by farmers, he also explained what agricultural labour and sugar cane cutters were going through.

In the night, we headed for Solapur. As we discussed in the afternoon meeting, the issue of farm labour cropped up. 'We just do not get labour. Right to Food Act and Employment Guarantee has led to this crisis. Today they think too much of themselves because of such sops by the state.' A leader of the Shetkari Sanghatana shared all that was pent up inside. It was a heated debate.

I was shocked by his logic on why there was a farm labour shortage.

What could I say?

Are labourers adamant? And do they refuse to work because of the food security and employment guarantee schemes? Do they actually think too much of themselves?

I was surprised, how weird!

This logic was not an individual opinion. It represented a myth that we had come across in many other places. I remembered one such event. People from one village used to labour in the pomegranate orchards in another village. So, there was a shortage of hands in their own village during onion harvesting. As an answer to this problem, the villages resolved no one would be allowed to work in other villages. They even tried to stop the vehicles that carried these labourers to the fruit orchards. The wages in the orchards are higher than what is paid for harvesting onion. The villagers did not think of increasing the wages as a solution. They could only come up with such bizarre restrictions on labour.

I could see no difference between those who blamed food security and employment guarantee for shortage labour and others who insisted that labourers work at lower wages. Both ran away from facts. Today's discussion made me ponder over that.

The Right to Food Act promises 25 kilograms of grain per family per month. The market value of this grain is 335 rupees which translates into 11 rupees per day for a family. A household of five members would get 2 rupees 23 paise. So, you mean to say that for these 2 rupees 23 paise, farm labourers are refusing work? What logic is this?

We saw a similar misconstrued position on the employment guarantee schemes. The Act says that it is mandatory to provide a minimum of 100 days of employment to anyone who demands it. In reality, people were hardly getting it even after solid agitation across the state. Wages are fixed at Rs. 203 per day. But that is rarely paid. And the delays are another blow.

The problem is not with the welfare schemes. It is about a fair wage that compensates the labour. And about the guarantee of regular and continuous availability of work.

Farming in Maharashtra is predominantly rainfed. We have been able to irrigate just 17 per cent of the cultivable land in the state. The remaining 83 per cent still depends on rain. This rainfed agriculture provides employment only for one season, only around sowing, planting, and harvesting. With the advent of smaller tractors, herbicides, hullers, and harvesters, even this employment is shrinking. Rainfed farming is no longer capable of creating regular and continuous employment for the farm labourers.

Irrigated farming and orchards can provide regular work. But only 17 per cent of land is under irrigation which can hardly provide enough employment for a large number of labourers. There is a parallel growth of non-farm sectors such as construction, education, and business in areas with irrigated farming. These too provide for regular work, and naturally, labour moves from farming to these other sectors.

This is the reality.

How do we retain labour in farming? We need impetus for agro-processing, chain value production, on-farm subsidiary occupations, and irrigation – bringing development in the farming sector – and bringing in labour. Restraining their movement or blaming them for wanting more wages will not work. Those advocating such positions need to understand the ground reality.

The landholding pattern of the state is starkly different from the national scenario. Almost all the regions of the state followed a ryotwari system in the pre-colonial era. We never had landlords having hundreds of acres of land. Most of the farmers are marginal farmers. Over the generations, land parcels have been increasingly divided into smaller plots making them unviable for farming. It is impossible to sustain by cultivating such small plots. Seventy-five per cent of farmers in this state are facing this.

The land was divided into smaller plots, and the line demarcating farmers and farm labourers blurred. Almost all the farmers have to tend to their land and then double time on someone else's farm or look for other wage labour. This is stark in rainfed and Adivasi areas. So, a binary of farmers and farm labourers does not work here. Blaming food security and employment guarantee schemes is far from reality as many farmers themselves need these schemes to survive. One has to understand these facts before taking any positions.

Farming is no longer viable thanks to state policies, among many other reasons. It is evident that more and more people want out. Many surveys have shown that given a better alternative, most farmers are willing to leave farming. Similarly, farm labourers, too, are searching and migrating for better options. Those who are still engaged in agriculture can't get out for want of such options.

The situation of these farmers trapped in farming is alarming. More so of the women labourers as seen in the status report on women farm labourers submitted by Prof. Balu Gore to the Swami Ramanand Teerth Marathwada University, Nanded. His survey shows that 93.5 per cent of women farm labourers were unable to fulfil even their basic needs from their wages, and 48.5 per cent of the women surveyed have taken a loan from a private money lender. Forty-seven per cent of women have backache, while 44.5 per cent of them complain of a stomach ache. A whopping 87 per cent report that due to poverty, they were not able to get adequate nutrition during pregnancy, and all, 100 per cent, had to do wage labour even when they were pregnant. The survey showed that 81 per cent of women reported their husband's addiction to alcohol, and 90 per cent had faced physical abuse from their alcoholic husband. Eighty-four per cent reported following some religious leaders or cult and their diktats.

This is very disturbing!

These women labourers were trapped and exploited in this vicious cycle of poverty, superstitions, ill-health, and injustice. The survey gave us an insight into how their families were coping. A survey of farmers in rainfed areas will throw up similar horrors. We addressed a meeting in Beed today. Thousands of farmers and labourers from this district migrate every year for working in sugar cane fields. Their situation is worse. The state has followed policies that are friendly to corporates and centred on cities. As a result, the entire farming sector is in shambles. For all those who do not have a way out – farming is proving to be a house of horror.

It is a just demand that farmers give a fair wage to their labourers. Women labourers in Marathwada receive a daily wage of Rs. 125 only, and there is no guarantee that they will find work throughout a month. How can one survive on such a paltry wage considering all the expenses on food, clothing, housing, health and education with increasing inflation? Therefore, labourers have to be paid a decent wage that honours their hard work. But the farmers can't pay such a wage as they themselves are in crisis. They are unable to earn enough to cover their costs of cultivation. So they are either trapped in debt or are choosing death. They cannot escape because of their land. And this lack of alternatives is pushing them farther down. Farmers are faced with a question: if they don't have money, how will they pay the labourers? There needs to be a guarantee of a fair price for a fair wage.

To ensure sufficient resources at source and distribution, one cannot move farther by thinking of farmers and farm labourers as separate entities. Both these groups are victims of the anti-farming policies of the state, and therefore, we need alternative approaches. The Swaminathan Commission knew this and took a comprehensive position. It has recommendations not just for farmers but for all the labourers in rural areas who may not own any piece of land. Along with MSP, the Commission recommends land for landless, food security for all, ownership of land to the tiller, the minimum wage for labourers, a comprehensive insurance cover for rural households, Price Stabilisation Fund, housing and healthcare, pension and education, livestock development, protection of the environment, and conservation of biodiversity.

Unions of farmers and farm labourers need to widen their positions on similar lines. Various governments have repeatedly exploited the farming sector to feed their corporate-friendly policies. Farmers and labourers struggle to get back what was theirs. These are also struggling to protest any such loot in the future. A demand for a loan waiver is not begging. The struggle is to end the loot, and it needs a united front of all the workers along with farmers and farm labourers. Activists and their organizations have to rethink their positions and adopt a balanced view. I sensed this very strongly on our way from Beed to Solapur.

The journey was arduous and distant.

And there was darkness – of prejudices and hypocrisy, of injustice and ignorance, of inequality and poverty, of pain and superstition – and darkness of exploitation, known and unknown.

And now we, the children of the tillers, were here to cut through this darkness!

Narsayya Adam, a leader of CPM and Siddhappa Kalshetti of Kisan Sabha had organized the Solapur rally on 21 July. Adam Master, as he is known fondly, has a vast network among workers and labourers in Solapur. We spent the night in the Godavari Parulekar Sankul, a unique housing project spearheaded by Adam Master and completed successfully by CITU. Ten thousand women beedi workers were provided with a house at highly subsidized rates in this huge colony. This is the biggest ever housing project of this kind in Asia. After the first phase, another one with 5,000 houses was completed. Master is now working day and night to complete the third phase of 30,000 houses. He wants to utilize grants under the PMAY (Pradhan Mantri Avas Yojana). H. A. Sheikh, Nalini Kalburgi, Naseema Sheikh, Siddhappa Kalshetti, Yusuf Major, and many others are working night and day to fulfil this dream. Adam Master has put in all the goodwill that he earned through his lifelong commitment to people. The man simply knows no bounds! It is not just his confidence but also some solid support of beedi workers, power loom workers, autorickshaw drivers, Anganwadi workers, construction workers and their strong unions that makes him so. Despite all that, this three-term MLA from Solapur faced defeat in the 2009 and 2014 elections. We are at a loss for words.

What rules here in this democracy is money, caste and religion. This democracy belongs to them.

So be it.

Really?

The Solapur event saw a lot of farmers who had constructed polyhouses on their farms. We keep hearing numerous success stories of farmers using modern technology on their farms and earning handsome profits. Young farmers with polyhouse and shade net houses on their farms are often the heroes of such success stories. And we believe that they have overcome the crisis and are content with their lives. But the reality is no way close. The state policies and the natural calamities have been detrimental to their growth. The agrarian crisis has crippled them. Inconsistent state policies, recurring drought, climate change, and natural disasters have pushed them into huge debts. These loans, often with compound interest, are a massive burden. And the so-called success stories have turned into tragedies. Even if they decide to sell their farmland, with the polyhouse on it, they won't be able to pay their debts.

What were their demands? They know that their government acts with compassion when it writes off the pending loans of industry and businesses. They want their loans to be waived in these times of crisis. They want full insurance cover for the polyhouse crops, the polythene paper, and the entire structure; safeguard for their perishable produce against the volatile market, and a policy for price control on-farm inputs such as pesticides, fertilizers, fungicides, and the seeds. These are fair demands, and these farmers had come to Solapur hoping that the Sukanu Samiti would include these in its agenda. Sanjay Talekar, a polyhouse farmer from Solapur, led their contingent.

49

The next programme was at Sangli. The lead organizers were Umesh Deshmukh of Kisan Sabha and Mahesh Kharade from the Swabhimani Shetkari Sanghatana. Farm leaders from the region spoke at the event, and the discussion around dairy was meaningful. The issue of milk pricing was unresolved for decades as there was no long-term policy for that. The government announces a short-term subsidy to try and diffuse the issue. But the problem persists. The dairy farmers are agitated and demand a long-term solution and a comprehensive policy in this regard.

What are some comprehensive measures that the farmers are waiting for?

A seventy-to-thirty revenue sharing policy. Procurement of whole milk to eradicate malnutrition in children. An end to the brand-wars, programmes that support healthy competition. The create an impetus for processing plants through milk co-operatives, strengthening the chain of value addition, strict monitoring for avoiding adulteration, ban on toned milk, a law to control profiteering by milk federations and private milk companies. The share of profit for the milk producers and their families should increase, reduction in the cost of production, alternative solutions in case of a ban on plastic bags for milk, a law to monitor the nutrition value and quality of cattle feed, modern technology to boost production, promotion for exports, and a price stabilisation fund. These constitute a comprehensive solution for the issues faced by the dairy farmers.

But our rulers were busy catching those in opposition who had some hold over the milk trade. Those high up in the business were profiteering with international milk powder prices and state subsidies. The administration was bothered about their 'cut' in these subsidies. The milk-producing farmer was alone in her fight with low prices, droughts, and apathy of the various stakeholders. The milk-producing farmers needed to organize themselves, and shatter this apathy and self-centeredness. The programme at Sangli left this strong urge in us. Now, we were headed towards Kolhapur.

Leaders and activists from Shetkari Sanghatana, PWP, and Kisan Sahba had organized the Kolhapur event. Namdev Gavade, Sampat Bapu Pawar-Patil, and Subhash Nikam had managed a good mobilization. We were in the land of sugarcane, and not just the crop but the agitations and protests by Raju Shetty around that crop.

Every crushing season, the sugar belt of the state is up in arms for a fair amount of the advance payment. The issue has gotten complicated since it was linked to sugarcane's Fair and Remunerative Price (FRP). The problems of the sugarcane growers have solutions: a fair import-export policy; a fair system for the sale of sugar, ethanol, and other by-products; and an end to corruption and mismanagement in the sugar factories. This will do justice to the farmers and also pacify the unrest. We were convinced of this as we spoke with the farmers at Kolhapur.

The culmination programme was planned at Pune. Amol Waghmare and Natha Shingade of Kisan Sabha, Dr Baba Adhav of Hamal Panchayat, and Ganesh Jagtap from Shetkari Sanghatana had put in all their efforts to make it a grand success.

50

Sukanu Samiti had pushed for a guaranteed fair price for crops on the agenda along with the demand for a loan waiver. Some intellectuals were questioning how the left parties could support such a demand.

The critiques claimed that a fair price for food crops would result in a price rise, which will affect crores of people who will starve. They also believed that this demand serves the interests of the wealthy farmers and does no good to the small and marginal farmers. They objected that, as Marxists, we could not take this position.

The truth is that the demand for a fair price is not only for wealthy farmers. It applies to everyone who wants to sell their produce in the market. They were not asking for a favour. The state intervenes in the market in the name of controlling inflation. Using the Essential Commodities Act reduces the prices for agricultural produce, and farmers suffer losses. The guise is of how inflation hits the poor. But the benefits are for the big corporates, traders, agents, and exporters. This loot is legal. The demand for a support price saves them from this kind of exploitation. The critiques failed to understand this innate logic and construed the MSP as a dole. This is where they made a mistake.

Let's also ask ourselves. Do the farmers ever get a support price? Does the state put enough procurement centres that off a support price in place? The critiques do not go there. The situation on the ground is pathetic. These were mere announcements. Barring a few centres, there is hardly any procurement. The farmers get a pittance compared with the gigantic loot over the years.

The critiques also faltered when they questioned how the state could procure the entire produce at the support price. This was impossible, they claimed. But our demand never meant that the state alone has to procure. It was misconstrued.

We demanded that policies for import and export, agro-processing, marketing, value-addition, sale, and cost of cultivation should be such that the farmers will get a fair price anywhere in the market. The state should have to intervene only as an exception. On the one hand, the state should procure foodgrains at support price for ensuring food security for the poor, and on the other, it should have policies for a fair price for farm produce. Both the policies should go hand in hand.

Today, farming is unviable, but processing and marketing are reaping good profits. We have to increase the participation of farmers in these profit-making sectors, thereby ensuring a price for their produce in the market.

It is ironic that in the farming sector, a producer has to purchase the 'input' at a 'higher' retail price and sell the produce 'lower' and 'wholesale' rates. This does not make any sense in economic terms. We have to turn this upside down. The farmers should get the farm inputs such as seeds, fertilizers, pesticides, etc., at wholesale rates. With increased facilities for storage and efforts at value addition, linkages with consumers, processing, and capital investment, a farmer should be able to sell the farm produce at retail prices. This will reduce the cost of production, and farmers will earn better. It is possible to build such systems through farmers' collectives, group farming, and farmer producer companies. It needs people's participation and state support. This is necessary if farmers are to get a fair price for their produce.

Minimum support price based on the cost of production is

only viable when the cost is reduced. And that will happen only when profiteering by the giant companies stops. Research from the agriculture universities and advancement in technology can accelerate lowering the cost of production.

We have to expand how we look at farming. It starts with the soil and reaches the consumer's doorstep. To ensure that a farmer gets a minimum support price – we need electricity, irrigation, roads, cold storage facilities, reliable and accurate weather forecasts, research and development of infrastructure. We also need insurance, credit, and a system of using the crop as a surety. All this will ensure that farmers get a fair price for their produce even in the market. Our demand was based on this logic, and we were putting that across in the Sukanu Samiti events.

51

We reached Pune on 22 July for the culmination event of our tour. Amol Waghmare, Dr Dnyaneshwar Mote, Dr Maharudra Dake, and Natha Shingade came and met us in the morning. They are a fantastic team, active and willing to learn, constantly pushing for constructive action on the field along with agitations.

Amol Waghmare is an activist with a quiet and calm composure, ever willing to help those in need. A good person and a good friend. Amol has been doing solid work in Ambegaon taluka of Pune district. With help from his friend circle, he has started many endeavours, including a library, a clinic, an ambulance service, and a night school to name a few. He organizes health camps, works for employment generation, and is engaged in water conservation, soil health, and numerous initiatives. Maharudra is involved in these activities as well.

I got acquainted with Maharudra when I was studying in Pune. I was from a communist background but got introduced to RSS groups in Pune and began attending the Shakha, reciting *namaste sada vatsale*,[5] following all that came with it. I was active in the Akhil Bharatiya Vidyarthi Parishad (ABVP). The SFI and ABVP collectively organized many agitations during that time. So, I came to Maharudra and his group. They were a dedicated lot, be it in a campaign or a debate. They were in it entirely, wholly devoted to their work. It was incredible.

Students from rural backgrounds face many difficulties while studying in cities and urban settings. From food habits and lifestyle to language, manners, and cultural differences, they face a thousand problems. Against this backdrop, I was trying to form alliances regarding problems students encountered in their hostels, issues regarding scholarships, and the non-availability of sufficient teachers. I used to meet one and all with the aim to build state-wide pressure on the government regarding these issues. My interest in coordinated campaigns is not new.

Dr Maharudra Dake and Shekhar Bendre worked in the SFI. The Tilak Ayurved College in Pune was known as the SFI bastion. I was from ABVP, but we knew that we could not build enough pressure unless both organizations came together. We talked to many people from these groups, begged them to join hands, and formed an action committee. In a state-wide campaign, such action committees were formed in forty-two colleges. Many local-level campaigns followed with district meetings and rallies. The culmination event was in Mumbai.

We had prepared well for the Mumbai march. Ten thousand students had gathered. In those days, marches in Mumbai were not banned. Ours was a massive rally from Azad Maidan to Mantralaya. Terrific! It was stopped at Kala Ghoda, near Mantralaya. Our delegation went to meet the ministers. It was my first time to go inside the Mantralaya in a delegation. It was the BJP government, and Dr Daulatrao Aher was the health minister. Even after a lot of discussions, nothing fruitful came out. So, we decided to go on a

---

[5] RSS prayer.

hunger strike. Ten students were asked to sit on a hunger strike at Kala Ghoda. Being an ABVP member, I used to think that the BJP government was 'our' government, and they will find a solution. Four days passed without a solution in sight. Due to incessant rains, everything was wet, including the footpath where we sat for the hunger strike – mosquitoes, biting cold and disregard. We were in utter distress!

Maharudra was always there with me through these agitations. We used to discuss numerous issues. God. Religion. Nation. State. Poverty. Exploitation. Caste. Reservation. The list was unending. We used to chat for hours, spending sleepless nights and talking all through the nights. Our minds were full of questions, especially about the existence of god and humankind. Of birth and rebirth. Of the origin of the universe. Of reasons behind poverty. Of Ramayana, Mahabharat and The Puranas. We discussed till we found answers. ABVP egged us to feel proud of one's origin and the purity of our lineage. The pride about one's religion, nation, race, history, and the notions of superiority about one's culture rode high in these discussions. Maharudra would share something very different – about the origin of the human being, of mixing of races. On how god and religion came into being. He also talked about the crux of exploitation. It used to shock me, and many of the prejudices would be shaken. One day, he gave me *From Volga To Ganga* authored by Rahul Sankrityayan. I read it fervently – not once, not twice, but thrice! And I was shaken. That book busted so many myths in my mind – how humankind evolved, how god was created. Human groups. Clans. State. Nation. Country. Culture. Hunting. Foodgrain. Farming. Metals. Tools. Customs. Kin. Marriage. Family. Vedas. Soul. Divine. Literature. Stories. Tales. Purana. Scriptures. History. Dualism. Darshan. Chaturvarnya. Chaturashram. Detachment. Slavery. Exploitation. Belief in god. It was almost as if a door opened into a new enlightened world. It made me calm. The inner turmoil reduced. The false pride in one's blood fell off. Being born in a particular religion or caste was a biological accident. The satisfaction I took in that felt petty. I began drifting away from the RSS and ABVP ideologies. I felt an innate solid urge to read more, know more, and examine my own beliefs.

The struggle was on – inside and out in the open.

The state had neglected our agitation. The ABVP leadership was not willing to fight it till the end. This was when SFI took full charge. The Hutatma Chowk would be blocked on the fourth day of the hunger strike. We were ready. And students started the *rasta roko* at 5 pm in the Hutatma Chowk. They were not more than two-three hundred students. But they held each other tightly and slept right there, on the road. The traffic light turned green, vehicles started moving, and it was a jam. 5 pm. The workers from companies nearby had left offices. The roads had full traffic. At a stone's throw, the Assembly session was underway. The timing was perfect.

Everything came to a standstill: the Assembly and all the crossroads in the vicinity. And then began the arrests. And then, jail. Seventy of us were in jail. Maharudra, too, lodged in the next cell. The government was now ready for discussion. The power of our agitations made sure that all our demands were met. The hunger strike was called off. We were waiting for our leaders from ABVP to come and release us. They didn't. No help came our way as we had got 'our' government in trouble. I was deeply hurt. It took me farther away from RSS and ABVP. I came into the folds of SFI. Maharudra has been a friend since then.

In the wee hours of 3 June, as I barged out of the CM's residence, these memories came back strongly. I was in a hurry and was almost running, but I had called Maharudra to narrate the previous night's events. I relived those moments today, and I felt alive. All the memories surged back. Most of them are good. They give you strength and energy. They remind you of the meaning of life.

The entire team – Ajit Abhyankar, Amol, Dnyaneshwar, Maharudra, Shubha Shamim, Vasant Pawar, and all the comrades from Pune came and met us before the sabha. They were thrilled, and the preparations were on. It felt like home.

52

23 July 2017. It was the last day of the statewide campaign of Sukanu Samiti, where farmers have mobilized once again for a long struggle. We needed to announce our call for struggle in the culmination event at Pune. I had tried to bring everyone on a common ground on this. Members of the Sukanu Samiti had discussed it in Amaravati, where many options were considered. Kisan Sabha had proposed a chakka jam across the state. But Raghunath Patil and Kalidas Apet toed a different line. They proposed not letting the guardian ministers hoist the flag on 15 August, Independence Day. They claimed that this would pressure the government to accede to our demands.

Kisan Sabha was firmly opposed to any agitation against the national flag. For us, it represents our love for this nation. Apet and Patil were adamant about their stand. They were willing to put our unity in danger but were determined to continue with their idea of protest. We had delayed a decision till our culmination event in Pune.

We had to come to a unanimous decision regarding our proposed campaign. Baba Adhav was present for the Sukanu meeting for the first time. We began discussing our future actions. I proposed an indefinite chakka jam. Raghunath Patil continued with his plan of disallowing flag hoisting at the hands of the guardian ministers. It looked like Patil and Apet had convinced Baba and other members of their idea. Many members were taking an opportunistic stand. These were comrades to us. I was pleading with them not to get into anything linked with the national flag as it would give BJP a chance to shift focus from loan waiver to patriotism. Dr Dhawale was going to attend the culmination event a bit late, so he was not present for this meeting. Anil Dethe, Kisan

Gujar, Rohidas Dhumal, and Santosh Wadekar were firmly behind me. But Raghunath Patil was hell-bent on his plan. To mediate, I suggested that we do a chakka jam on 14 August and on the Independence Day, we should insist that a farmer hoist the flag.

This proposal irked Raghunath Patil. He almost jumped from his chair. 'You can go ahead with chakka jam, if you wish. But we will not let the guardian minister hoist the flag!' he roared.

What could anyone say now? The meeting ended.

We were not happy with the decision as it was not the right thing to do. We started towards the venue with a heavy heart. Now the government had all reasons to defame the movement. Many senior leaders such as Bhai Jayant Patil, Dr Ashok Dhawale, Baba Adhav and Bachchu Kadu were present. Most of the Sukanu Samiti members were there. Raju Shetty was conspicuous in his absence. Swabhimani Sanghatana was not very active in the entire campaign. At the outset, Raghunath Patil had passed a comment in front of the media: *Naav swabhimani, kaam beimaani* (they call themselves self-respecting, but their deeds are those of traitors) which had hurt them. Thus, Swabhimani Sanghatana decided not to participate.

I was not convinced about the decision, so I suggested that Patil make the announcement and requested him. He happily agreed. We all spoke at the gathering, explaining how the government was cheating the farmers. We appealed to everyone to join the farmer's movement.

The 14-day campaign had thus ended, and we were headed home. Events from the last two weeks, internal tussles, wanting to outdo the others, the meeting in the afternoon, adamant stand by our colleagues, and the culmination event . . . my mind kept repeating the events.

I was exhausted.

Inside, I knew very well that we needed a fresh start. The fatigue weighed heavy on me.

IV

53

All of us cherish the tri-colour and Independence Day. I was just not convinced of any action that would cause disrespect to these symbols of our love and reverence, but I could not override a collective decision. News of Sukanu Samiti's campaign had reached all across the state. The media was curious and eager to get the updates. I was the convener of Sukanu Samiti, and thus, people were keen to watch the events in Ahmednagar. I had no option but to gear up for it.

All the activists of Kisan Sabha had decided to concentrate only on the chakka jam planned on the 14 August. In Ahmednagar, I had to prepare both events well. So, I appealed to our sister organizations and started our work. In Akole, we started mobilizing youth around the theme, *Aamhi Saari Shetkaryanchi Pora* (We, the children of farmers). Lahanu Sadgir, Mahesh Navale, Nilesh Talekar, Rohidas Dhumal, Dr Sandip Kadlag, and Vilas Arote geared up for the events. Local journalists worked like activists, helping generously. The support came from all corners going beyond political identity. College youth participated actively, especially the girl students. We wanted the chakka jam in Akole to be a resounding success, so we fully immersed ourselves in it.

14 August 2017. The chakka jam protest in Akole was a huge success. Eight thousand young farmers came out on the streets. The event was compelling. Across the state, Kisan Sabha led the agitations in twenty-three districts, with more than 85,000 farmers participating in the chakka jam. Many other organizations came out in support. More than two lakh farmers protested all across

the state. This chakka jam showed us again that the campaign has yet to lose steam.

We needed to follow the decision and protest on 15 August. Rather than opposing the entire event, we decided to oppose flag hoisting by the guardian minister selectively and insisted that it should be at the hands of a farmer. The main event in Ahmednagar was planned at the district headquarters. We had to get there by 7 am. We had an inkling that the police might put a few key activists under arrest in their own blocks. Considering all such possibilities, we decided that all key persons should spend the night in Ahmednagar at unknown locations. After successfully implementing chakka jam in Akole on 14 August, I headed towards Nashik to participate in a panel discussion on Sam TV. Khandubaba accompanied me. As always, Sanjay Awate conducted a spirited debate on the farmers' issues. I reached Ahmednagar at 2 am. Fellows from Akole had arrived as well.

Knowing that police might arrest us, we decided to stay in separate rooms. I chose a dingy place to stay, and Khandubaba joined me. Ajay Maharaj Baraskar is an activist with Prahar Sanghatana. He is known for his Kirtan. He was in the next room. The police came early in the morning and raided his room. Other activists raised slogans as they were taken to the vehicles. We woke up and stayed awake. Our activists played smart and did not indicate our whereabouts in any manner.

We immediately got ready as our plan was in place. Two people were sent down to check whether police were around. Two of them were waiting in the next hotel. A vehicle was kept ready at a distance. They may not have known that we were around. They just took a chance, I suppose. Usually, I am at the wheel. But this time, I had a driver with me. We got in the car and started towards Akole instead of Nagar as police had kept a tight vigil on all vehicles coming towards Nagar. We were driving in the opposite direction. After driving for two kilometres, we changed our route. No one followed us. We reached the Hutatma Smarak. All the activists had reached the memorial as planned. We were in the crowd.

Every year the freedom fighters and ex-servicemen gather at the Hutatma Smarak on the 26 January and 15 August. They hoist the flag and then join the flag hoisting programme conducted by the guardian minister. We had decided to participate in this event and then move towards the main event to protest as planned.

The flag hoisting started right on time. Jai Jawan! Jai Kisan! Bharat Mata Ki Jai! *Swatantrya Din Chirayu Hovo* (Long live Independence Day)! These spirited slogans filled the air. After flag hoisting and singing the national anthem, we came out of the Smarak as if we were taking out a celebratory morning rally. By then, police had received the intimation, and we saw at least 50-60 police officers on the road.

We started shouting slogans and swiftly went towards the main venue. We reached the gate, and hardly anybody knew that. The gate was closed. Many citizens were waiting to get in. We started our protest there. Jai Jawan! Jai Kisan! Our slogans roared. We also raised farmers' demands, and that led to big chaos. Police officials ran towards the entrance, and the situation became quite tense. They were in contact with their seniors. There was a significant media presence. Our activists were loud and vocal. Police were trying to push us back, and their vans were ready. Our arrest was imminent. But we were not to budge.

Then, it turned physical. The tension was palpable, and at that moment, the police held Dr Sandip Kadlag, my friend from Akole and a leader with Sambhaji Brigade. They were trying to get him into the van. A few more were held and taken towards their vehicle. Our activists were resisting. Police were trying to get hold of as many as they could. They called for additional force. We were picked up, put into their vehicles, arrested, and taken to the police stations far outside the city. In a moment, the news of our arrest spread like wildfire.

We spent the entire day at the station. Each one received just two bananas. Order to release us came in the evening. They took us in the police vans and left us far outside the main city. We had followed the collective decision of the Sukanu Samiti. It didn't matter if we agreed or not. The protest was held.

In the evening, I returned to Akole. As I gathered information on protests from other parts of the state, I was shocked. Raghunath Patil, who was resolute that come what may we will stop the guardian minister, had not organized any protest in his home district Sangli! Apparently, he went to the Government Rest House with just three activists. He met the guardian minister, exchanged a few words, and simply left without protest. Our Kisan Sabha activist from Sangli, Umesh Deshmukh, was arrested the night before and kept in jail till morning. Patil didn't even care to go and meet Umesh. Barring a few events, Raghunath Patil's followers did not organize any protests in any other district.

54

The CM took special cognizance of this. At a BJP regional executive committee meeting, he came down heavily, 'All those who oppose flag hoisting are anti-national! They are raising the slogan of a total loan waiver and are heading towards anarchy . . .! Media caught on this. Their screens showed an aggressive CM on one side, and on the other, it was me trying to create anarchy. This went on for the whole day.

The next day, all media channels were discussing nationalism and anarchy. I was called on the panel. The ground was set for a discussion. The border areas witnessed an Indo-China conflict, and I was a CPI(M) activist and the convenor of the Sukanu Samiti. It was the CM who had accused the Sukanu Samiti of being anti-national. The discussion was to happen on this backdrop. The farmers' movement had put the state government into the dock, and now they had got a chance to paint us as criminals. They were desperate. We, too, were ready.

The BJP spokesperson was trying everything to unsettle me.

But I kept calm. We never opposed Independence Day or the flag hoisting. Instead, we had participated in the Independence Day celebrations. Our only demand was that a farmer hoists the flag and not the guardian minister. How is this anti-national? We asked the BJP. We also reminded them that the RSS headquarters refused to hoist the national flag until recently. The media representatives were sensitive to the farmers' demands and gave us ample time to speak. The BJP was finding itself in a tight spot. CM's wish of diverting the discussion on farm issues to nationalism did not quite succeed. Still, we had to take the blame for being anti-national. That too for no reason. It was disturbing. And those who were responsible for this chaos were not in the picture at all. They might be watching all this from a distance and possibly enjoying it.

'Doctor, don't you think all this was staged?' Khandubaba raised a doubt.

55

The protests received a mixed response in various parts of the state. In Parbhani, it turned violent. Vehicles were attacked and damaged. Rasta roko, in many places, received an excellent response. Police blamed Vilas Babar and Rajabhau Rathod of Kisan Sabha for this entire episode. They were charged under dacoity and arrested. They were abused and harassed while in custody. Kisan Sabha did all it could to help them, and we needed to send a message that we stand firmly behind Vilas, Rajabhau, and all other activists. I needed to visit Parbhani. And thus, a meeting was planned there on the 29 August.

The meeting was arranged at the government rest house. All core members, including Dr Ashok Dhawale, Baba Adhav, Bachchu Kadu, Raghunath Patil, and Vishwas Utagi were present. Raju Shetty did not come. He had asked Manik Kadam, a leader of Swabhimani Shetkari Sanghatana from Parbhani to attend the meeting. Raghunath Patil's followers objected to his presence,

147

saying he was not a member of the Sukanu Samiti. It looked as if their sole agenda was to keep Raju Shetty out of Sukanu Samiti. We had to witness these unfortunate events in the farmers' movement.

After some tense moments, things cooled down, and we proceeded with our agenda. The meeting went well. We had organized a Shetkari Melava at Shrihari Mangal Karyalay, followed by a press conference. At both these events, we registered our protest against the arrests and police brutality in Sangli and Parbhani. It was decided that the Sukanu Samiti would organize a vast statewide congregation at Jalgaon. After the press conference, we went to the collector and submitted a memorandum marking our protest against the police atrocity in Parbhani. Many farmers had brought Bhakri and Kharda (a pungent green chilli and peanut chutney) with them for lunch. So, we sat down outside the collectorate and ate that meal along with hundreds of farmers. Dr Dhawale, Bachchu Kadu, Raghunath Patil, and prominent leaders from across the state shared this meal and protested along with the farmers. It did give a boost to all our activists.

Everything worked out well. But I sensed that something was amiss in the Sukanu Samiti. It was possible that a few members felt that they were not getting enough share of the leadership. It was evident from their body language. I shared this with Khandubaba as we headed towards Nagar.

56

Two days passed, and my feeling turned out to be true. We had created a WhatsApp group of Sukanu Samiti members for internal communication. On that group, Sanjay Ghatanekar posted a message regarding the next Sukanu meeting planned at Pandharpur on 7 September. Being a convenor, it was my job to coordinate with office bearers and plan and announce the meeting dates. This was an unwritten rule. And here, a meeting was fixed without consulting many other leaders or me. We had a meeting in

Parbhani just three days back, and there was no reason for another one immediately. All of us kept wondering why.

After some digging, many new events emerged. As the meeting at Parbhani got over, we returned to Nagar. Many other leaders headed back home. However, Ganesh Jagtap, Kalidas Apet, Kishor Dhamale, Raghunath Patil, and Sanjay Ghatanekar stayed back in Parbhani. They held another meeting in the night. Their strategy was to create another core group to increase their influence and take leadership. Eleven members from 40-45 state representatives were chosen for this new core committee. They had planned to intimate us later. They could not have left me out, so I was on the new committee. But Dr Ashok Dhawale, Bhai Jayant Patil, and Raju Shetty were left out. Bachchu Kadu was not included either. He along with Baba Adhav, were inducted as advisors. The whole episode was infuriating.

I talked in detail with all those who were part of this meeting. I tried my best to explain how creating a small committee of just 11 people would lead to discontent and factions within the movement. We will lose people's support, disturbing the unity and strength of the farmer's movement. But it seemed that our fellows were determined not to listen and pay heed. They were not bothered if their hunger for power and leadership would lead to a breakdown of the Sukanu Samiti. They were simply not bothered. Like Sheikhchilli, they chose to cut the branch they sat on.

57

Dr Dhawale was unavailable for the Pandharpur meeting as he was out of state. I was busy as my nephew was hospitalized a day before the meeting. On the one hand, I did not feel like attending this meeting as it was a divisive move, but the core committee would be announced anyway if I didn't go. Others who were kept out of the committee would feel hurt. And news about the 'division' or factions in the Sukanu would spread like wildfire.

I had had enough of this petty politics. I decided not to attend. I went to the hospital to be with my nephew. I was very much distressed. These leaders were interested more in their politics than the farmers' woes. I could not take it anymore.

I sat by my nephew's bedside until midnight to monitor the IV drops. My mind kept repeating the events from the farm strike to the recent developments. All our efforts to raise and strengthen the movement were now caught in the internal fights. The saline drops were over, and I lay down for a while. I tried very hard to catch some sleep, but I could not. The thoughts kept me awake and made me very restless. If I did not attend the meeting, the movement would suffer greatly.

Finally, at 2 am, I called up Khandubaba and told him that we had to go to Pandharpur. He had been down with a fever for the last three days. No other driver would come at such short notice. So, I had to drive all the way from Akole to Pandharpur, eight hours one way. I needed someone to accompany me. I convinced him that we had to go despite his health issues. We started at 3 am. The road was in an utter mess. The potholes and repair work had hauled traffic movement at many places. I had to reach on time, lest the news of the formation of a new core committee reaches the press. I would have to answer why Dr Dhawale, Bachhu Kadu, and Raju Shetty were not on the committee. I was trying to drive as fast I could. Khandubaba was by my side, down with fever and suffering.

Around 7 am, we stopped at one tea stall. The tea was very bitter, but we drank it somehow and started driving. The traffic snarls on the way were frustrating. I could not stop thinking about my nephew in the hospital. Khandubaba was also unwell, and I felt guilty to have made him travel with me. I kept driving, only for the unity of the Sukanu Samiti. We reached Pandharpur at 1 pm. Due to the traffic snarls, it took us more than ten hours instead of the usual eight.

The good thing was that the *melava* (gathering of people) was planned before our meeting. Who knows if this was because I was going to attend the meeting? Lunch was scheduled after the *melava*. So, I headed straight to the venue without any food since the morning.

It was supposed to be a big event, with at least five to seven thousand farmers attending it. Sanjay Ghatanekar has taken the responsibility of mobilizing. There were not more than 200 to 300 people. After some routine speeches, the event was over. All of us were disappointed.

From the venue, I came to the guest house and joined the meeting without eating. The issue of the Core Committee came up for discussion. I calmly opposed it again.

'The Sukanu Samiti was formed on the backdrop of the farmers' strike. We cannot afford this infighting about who is more important and prominent. We have to get everyone on board. Keeping Dr Dhawale, Bachchu Kadu, Bhai Jayant Patil, and Raju Shetty out of this committee is a suicidal move,' I asserted my position. There was a lot of discussion around it. As I stood firm on my stand, my colleagues had to drop the idea of this new core committee. I proposed that we review the preparation for the Jalgaon conference. Another shock was in store.

'Doctor, we are of the opinion that the Jalgaon conference should be cancelled.'

Why? I had lost it by now. They seemed to be enjoying it, though.

The decision to organize a statewide conference was taken in the Parbhani meeting. The conference was needed to strengthen Sukanu Samiti's efforts. Pratibha Shinde was going to co-ordinate the Jalgaon conference. Some members were dead against it. She had invited Raju Shetty as well. Some members had successfully used this to get Raghunath Patil into their camp. They claimed that the conference should be cancelled considering the upcoming Gram Panchayat elections. I was firm that the conference should be held. A lot of debate and discussions led to a few decisions. I proposed that a delegation go to Jalgaon and review the preparedness and people's participation in the elections. It should talk to many people and then come to a decision. In case the conference is cancelled, the next meeting of the Sukanu Samiti should be organized in Jalgaon. This was agreed upon. A delegation of Karan Gaykar, Kishor Dhamale, Sanjay Ghatanekar, and Sushila Morale planned to visit Jalgaon on 8 September. The meeting concluded.

We immediately started our return journey towards Akole. I was completely drained out. I had not slept a few nights, was on the road for the entire day, and the stress of this meeting had exhausted me. Khandubaba had no energy left either.

The roads were blocked. Again. So were my thoughts.

Dust everywhere, covering each and everything. Outside and inside. Everywhere.

I was fed up.

It took us five hours to reach Ahmednagar. A four-hour drive further to reach Akole. I was dozing off and could not drive further. I was worried about my nephew's health, so we could not stop over at Nagar. Finally, I stopped at a petrol pump and lay down inside the car. In a minute, I was asleep.

The strike. Loan waiver. Sukanu Samiti. Core Committee. The thoughts never stopped.

Two hours passed like minutes. At 3 am, we started towards Akole.

I simply could not see any light. The dark of the night swallowed me up.

The road ahead was getting more and more arduous. The ship was going astray. The cracks were getting wider. It was getting harder and harder to keep Sukanu in one place.

Dejected, I kept at the wheel, cutting through the darkness of the night. The dawn was not in sight yet.

I feared for Khandubaba's health. He had travelled with me despite his fever. But Khandubaba Waghchaure is a gutsy fellow, fighting the disease with all his might. He is in pink of his health at seventy – kind at heart and utterly genuine.

He is exceptionally proud of the food he grew on as a child. That food had no chemicals, and he is very proud of that. You can feel it when he talks about it. He is active in the farmers' clubs and regularly attends agricultural camps and seminars. Though he is not highly educated, he has obtained a lot of knowledge through sheer experience, participation in farmers' clubs, extensive travel, and reading.

Baba is a staunch supporter of *visha mukta sheti* (toxin-free farming). 'Modern agriculture introduced toxins to our food. We defeated hunger but lost on well-being. It gave rise to so many diseases. It was disastrous,' he asserts.

He is genuinely in awe of the fertility of the soil. 'The soil is alive. It is made up of millions of microbes. We have destroyed it with indiscriminate pesticides, making it infertile, lifeless,' Khandubaba shares his angst.

'Soil gives us food; we too need to give it back to the soil. We take out the edible parts of the crop like grain and fruit. What remains is what we need to give back to the soil, the chaff, dry litter, dehusked cobs, etc. We have to let this decompose and help increase and enrich the carbon content of the soil. We have to bring life into it through microbes and other organizms', he explains. Khandubaba has a rare gift of breaking down profound philosophies in simple local terms.

'Excessive use of insecticides killed the honeybees, butterflies, and millions of insects which carry out pollination. We made sure that flowers were not pollinated and productivity spiralled down. We started using new chemicals newer fertilizers by newer companies to boost it. Our farming got trapped in these costly inputs and toxins,' he explains.

He tries all that he can to reverse and repair this. Travelling with him gives me these opportune moments to understand such processes. I find hope in him, energy that revives me when I am exhausted or down with hopelessness. My family, too, is relieved when they know that he is with me.

Khandubaba has been an old proponent of a united front of farmer's unions. Recently, many such unions were trying to form a national alliance. Khandubaba was very happy with these efforts. In the beginning, more than 200 unions and organizations were part of this collective. Those leading this effort included Hannan Mollah, the General Secretary of the AIKS, Raju Shetty of Swabhimani Shetkari Sanghatana, V. M. Singh of Kisan Union, Yogendra Yadav of Swaraj Abhiyan, and others. Khandubaba believed that the Sukanu Samiti should co-ordinate with this national coordination committee. I agreed with that. Avik Saha had called me on behalf of the Co-ordination Committee (AIKSCC). Sunilam, a farm leader from Madhya Pradesh had contacted me as well.

We were trying to get our constituent organizations to agree on such collaboration. And this could be done at the Sukanu Samiti meeting organized for the Jalgaon conference. AIKS, Pratibha Shinde's Lok Sangharsh Morcha, Raju Shetty's Swabhimani Shetkari Sanghatana, and Sushila Morale's Shetkari Samiti had joined the AIKSCC, and many others from Sukanu were willing. Many of us wanted to have Samanvay Samiti (Co-ordination Committee) at the national level and Sukanu Samiti at the state.

The preparations for the Jalgaon conference on 26 September were in full swing. Pratibha Shinde had worked tirelessly for that. Other local organizations too had contributed their own time and effort. Sukanu Samiti held a meeting before the conference. Raju Shetty was at the rest house's venue but did not join our meeting. Hansraj Wadgule and Ravikant Tupkar represented him.

We proposed to discuss the issue of collaboration with AIKSCC. Pratibha Shinde and Raju Shetty were members of the committee, which made some of our members insecure. They shared their inability to join such an alliance, saying they were part of other such collectives at the national level. They did not relent even after many requests. So, we had to forego the idea of any such collaboration at the national level. As the next step in our campaign, we decided to organize a huge *Baliraja gaurav miravanuk* (peasant felicitation rally) on the occasion of the upcoming Bali Pratipada (during Diwali).

The Jalgaon conference had massive participation by farmers. They were bursting with enthusiasm. We heard some powerful speeches. Overall, it was a successful conference. But it was getting more and more difficult for the Sukanu Samiti to hold its fort.

59

The efforts to build unity among all the farmer organizations and unions were commendable and genuinely in the interest of the farmers. But it was not easy to get all the members of Sukanu Samiti to join AIKSCC. A meeting was planned in Delhi towards such coordination, and Hannan Mollah and Dr Dhawale represented Kisan Sabha. I was invited on the backdrop of the farm agitation in Maharashtra. I was pretty keen to understand the developments in Delhi, and thus, I decided to attend the meeting.

Dr Dhawale, Pratibha Shinde, Raju Shetty, Sushila Morale, and I were in Delhi for the meeting. But some of our friends here in Sukanu did not like this. They announced a tour in Vidarbha without consulting anyone of us. There was no such decision taken in the Jalgaon meeting. Still, it was planned, and some select members went on this Vidarbha tour.

After this, Raghunath Patil called some national leaders and organized a conference in Pune from 10 to 13 December. Some participant organizations were invited to participate in this event.

This was not enough. They announced a political party of farmers. They also announced that the next meeting of the Sukanu Samiti was to be held in Aurangabad. Raghunath Patil and Kalidas Apet held a press conference at Aurangabad and announced it. Many dailies carried the news that Raghunath Patil was about to announce the formation of a new political party of farmers.

We were shocked by this turn of events. I was the state coordinator of Sukanu Samiti, and it was me who should announce a meeting. We witnessed these arbitrary decisions by members who had stopped following any norms or protocols beginning with the meeting at Pandharpur. Another concern was that members of Sukanu Samiti had different political views. The fact was that we had transgressed these political beliefs to come together and form an alliance on the issues of loan waiver, fair price for farm produce, etc. In fact, many political parties and their leaders and farmers had supported our struggle because we were not adamant about our political stand, and we were not here for our narrow political interests was our strength. Against this backdrop, talk of a new political party was completely out of line. To push for such a political entity was to end the existence of the Sukanu Samiti.

Many amongst us had demanded that we convert the Sukanu Samiti into a political outfit. Those who propagated this idea were the ones without any mass base. They were riding high on the success of the farmers' strike and were dreaming of being MLA or MP. They were egging Raghunath Patil to form an outfit saying 'Dada, announce a third alternative. People are waiting for us.' Patil never uttered a word about converting the Sukanu Samiti into a political outfit. But the discussion around the idea pointed towards that. The strike was under the slogan: Kisan Kranti. Sukanu Samiti's logo also had this tagline, gaining widespread support. Patil mentioned that the new outfit could well be called Kisan Kranti Dal in the Aurangabad conference. The indication was clear. At the Sukanu Samiti meeting on 22 December, he was to announce this.

Many of us were trying to resist this as strongly as we could. Some preferred to wait and watch, and some were being purely opportunistic. By now, we had realized that our resistance was not powerful enough. Bachchu Kadu, B. G. Kolse Patil, Bhai Jayant Patil, had almost stopped attending the meetings. So, there was not much that I could do even if I went to the Aurangabad meeting. I decided not to go. Many of the members skipped this meeting for their own reasons.

60

Two major decisions were made in the Aurangabad meeting. It was decided that henceforth, each Sukanu meeting will have a new chairperson, and the one selected for that meeting will talk to the media and inform them about the decisions.

It was out in the open that the first decision was to restrict my rights. As the convenor, I planned all the meeting dates, coordinated with all members, and finalized the agenda. It was natural that I also conducted the meetings. But now, with these decisions, these members were free to call for meetings, make decisions, talk to media, and form core committees as per their wishes.

The second decision was simply ridiculous – the limits of childishness. It was decided that farmers would go on another strike from 1 March for their demands.

This decision belittled the idea of the farmers' strike. The fire and energy behind the 1 June agitation had mellowed, almost died down. Farmers had suffered huge losses as their produce was not allowed to reach urban markets. They could not afford another loss. Also, none of the mass-based organizations was present in this meeting where this decision to go on a strike was made. Going ahead with such an important decision without consulting them was an immature act. The decision was not to go down well with many.

We saw very sharp reactions in Nashik, which emerged as the new centre for farmers' agitations after the Puntamba strike. The Sukanu Samiti was hardly being inclusive in its functioning lately. And this had angered many activists in Nashik. There was a feeling that others were appropriating their efforts of forming the Sukanu Samiti. The Aurangabad meeting was the last straw. A handful of people announced a strike without consulting other members. There was no thought given to our preparedness. The farmers were not consulted at all. They simply announced the date for the strike – 1 March 2018.

March is a busy month for grape growers in Nashik. School exams are held in the same month. People were outraged that these issues were not factored in. A preparatory meeting for the strike was planned for 1 January 2018 at Nashik. This angered many. One, they were not consulted while making the decision, and on top of that, the meeting to plan the strike was planned in their city. This was an insult.

I started getting many phone calls opposing the decisions made in the Aurangabad meeting, most of which were from Nashik. I was conveying this anger and resistance to the Sukanu Samiti members. The decision to go on a strike indeed needed a rethink. I was trying for the Nashik activists to express their views in the preparatory meeting rather than rejecting the idea of strike outright. But the situation was out of control as none of them was ready to listen. Many past events had angered them, and now, this decision to go on a strike brought out all that.

And it was going to explode.

Finally, Hansraj Wadgule from the Swabhimani Shetkari Sanghatana took the lead. He got together Ganesh Kadam, Karan Gaykar, and Raju Desale and held a press conference on 30 December. None of the Kisan Sabha activists was involved. He attacked the functioning of the Sukanu Samiti and was clinical in dissecting the decision of another strike. 'After the strike at Puntambe last year, we had formed the Sukanu Samiti in Nashik, and today we are dissolving that committee,' he announced in the press conference.

The decision to dissolve the Sukanu Samiti was all over the news the next day.

62

It was a sorry state of affairs, and it served well for those in power. The loan waiver scheme never helped because of the terms and conditions. And now the Sukanu Samiti, which was strong support for farmers, was counting its last breaths. I was not ready to give up and wanted to give it a last try. Dr Dhawale had agreed to come for the January meeting. I, along with Anil Dethe from Bhumiputra, Khandubaba, Kisan Gujar, Rohidas, Santosh Wadekar, and Vittha Pawar from the Sharad Joshi Vichar Manch, had decided to push for solidarity among our members.

The mood was damp and tense in Nashik. Those present for the meeting were resentful with a sense of bitterness in their minds. Following the decision at Aurganbad, Pratibha Shinde was selected as the chair for today's meeting. It looked as if everything was planned beforehand, and clearly, I was on their target, and the reason was that I had insisted that everyone, including Raju Shetty, should be part of the Sukanu Samiti. Nashik faction resisted and rebelled against the decision, which led to chaos. No sense prevailed. I had to face this without getting agitated. Anil Dethe and Santosh Wadekar from Bhumiputra Sanghatana, Rohidas Dhumal, and many others spoke in my support but in vain.

After a lot of debate and chaos, Dr Dhawale intervened. He minced no words and exposed the real faces of many. Insisting on the need to come together, he called out the leaders and said,

'Enough of your politics. The farmers have high hopes from our solidarity. Be mindful of that . . .!' People calmed down a bit after his speech, and we moved to discuss our issues, keeping aside hurtful sentiments. We engaged in a serious discussion after a while. The decision of the strike was reversed. Instead, we decided to follow the principle of non-cooperation.

We resolved the contentious issue of the strike. But Raghunath Patil came up with another one. He insisted that we should go and meet the Chief Minister. We were not willing as there was no invitation. But he was not convinced and declared a date for such a meeting. I was hurt and sad as the decision-making was no longer inclusive. I returned to Akole feeling dejected.

63

A handful of people now controlled the Sukanu Samiti. They failed to realize that they were digging a grave for themselves. Many left the Samiti as it was no longer a shared space, and many chose to be inactive. But, as Kisan Sabha, we were determined to face the situation and remain a part of the Sukanu Samiti.

We received a message saying, 'reach Mumbai to meet the CM, as planned'. It also said that Raghunath Patil had got an appointment. We resisted the idea of meeting the CM without any invitation. But remaining absent would have meant that we no longer belonged to the Sukanu Samiti. So, against all my wishes, I reached Mumbai on 16 January to meet the CM. Just before the meeting, we were told that the CM was not present in Mantralaya. Our visit was a waste of time.

After a few days, we were told that Raghunath Patil had taken another appointment. We went to Mumbai. The CM was at Sahyadri, but he simply greeted us without giving us much time as there was no formal invitation for a meeting from his side. There was no discussion. His actions made it clear that he hardly gave any importance to Sukanu Samiti.

'One should learn to deal with insult' was a message that Gandhiji gave. But here was a demonstration of how to initiate one's humiliation. In my mind, I was determined not to be part of any such fiasco in the future.

Some of us were bouncing with joy as they felt that they were the ones who controlled the Sukanu Samiti. They dreamed of becoming state-level leaders by simply touring the state. Even after being snubbed by the CM, they announced the state-wide tour. It was decided to hold a camp for activists from all organizations to prepare for this tour. They announced their plan to tour the entire state with thousands of followers and commemorate those who sacrificed their lives for this land. They held no bar and announced that they would fight all 288 assembly states in the 2019 elections after this tour.

We had completely lost it now. The decision to fight 288 seats was nothing but laughable. There was no point in protesting it. For them, loan waiver for farmers was no longer on the agenda. They were daydreaming about who will fight which seat. We had to find another way of taking our agitation to the next level. Young farmers went on a strike to free their parents from debt. We had to respect their emotions.

64

The loan waiver was announced seven months back. Most of the farmers were yet to receive any relief. The unending announcements and numbers, terms and conditions, and the online mode of filling forms had made sure that the farmers could not avail fresh loans either. The long list of terms and conditions was bound to keep most farmers out of the scheme.

The CM had claimed that the loan waiver was to benefit 89,87,000 farmers, but only 56,59,187 farmers were able to apply for the scheme. The terms and conditions of the scheme ensured that a whopping 33,27,813 farmers simply could not register and were thrown out, right in the first phase of the scheme.

The government had announced that the farmers had a collective debt of 1,14,000 crores. The loan waiver would waive 34,000 crores of the total debt, which means that farmers were still under a collective debt of 80,000 crores. Only 29.82 per cent of total debt was to be waived off.

But, on the other hand, the corporate sector has received a total waiver in taxes and debts amounting to more than 11,00,000 crores. The companies get into debt for their business failures. This is not caused by a natural disaster or state policies. The RBI hardly ever objects when such loans are waived off, or there is no debate over fiscal discipline or prudence. But when it comes to farmers, people bring up these issues of fiscal discipline and prudence. The educated young farmers were troubled by these discriminatory practices of banks, heads of financial institutions, and the overall system.

During the farmers' strike, we had very strongly pushed our demand for MSP that is no less than one and half times the cost of production. There was no concrete step taken towards this as well. The strike also brought the critical issue of milk rates to the fore. That remained unresolved. We had no choice but to hit the streets for these demands. But Sukanu Samiti no longer served that purpose. I had lost my sleep thinking about these issues.

65

The CPI(M) state conference was planned in Sangli on 15 February 2018. Many of us were there. Sitaram Yechury addressed a massive gathering and flagged off the conference. The next three days were quite busy for us, Kisan Sabha activists. Our leaders were to join the national conference. The Sukanu Samiti had selected the same period for the Hutatma Abhivadan Yatra (Martyr Commemoration Rally), ensuring that none of us could participate. The rally was to begin from Sangli on the same day that our state conference was organized. This seemed like a planned 'coincidence' deliberately mocking us.

Hutatma Abhivadan Yatra was an ambitious idea by Raghunath Patil, Kishor Dhamale, Kalidas Apet, and Ganesh Jagtap. It was almost like a candidate hunt for all the 288 assembly seats. The Yatra was to visit memorials of martyrs from the freedom struggle and peasants' movement. It was as if the hordes of prospective candidates would welcome the yatra in each district. At least five rallies with 10,000 people followed by a travelling troupe of 5000 people. A state-wide campaign on a whirlwind. The next CM was from our camp. Endless imagination!

But I ask, do you not need some sense of reality? Are we realistic about our strengths? Are we not trying to bite too much? These people were busy the whole last month drumming about their rallies. Fine. No one will stop you.

We were just about to culminate the first day of our convention. The Sukanu Samiti Yatra had taken off. We heard that fifty people were flagging off the yatra. F-i-f-t-y! This was only the preview of what was to come, all across the state. We could no longer look up to Sukanu Samiti to fight for our rightful loan waiver demand.

Just before dinner that day, we were sitting in a circle for a discussion. Comrade Jeeva Pandu Gavit came looking for us and then joined us.

MLA Gavit is a man of calm, quiet, and alert composure. He was elected for seven terms and had worked in the Party and Kisan Sabha in many capacities. But no airs about that. He lived very simply, and you could see him in a crowd of farmers and activists. It was no different in his constituency. He was one among the people. His fight for the farmers' rights was inspiring and helped countless families survive through the crisis. And not just farming, he had completed many water conservation projects and was instrumental in starting educational institutes. People simply loved him. He had built a strong organization. He was truly a people's leader. And all of us had great respect for him.

He came and joined us in our discussion. He hit the nail on the head.

'It is high time we leave the Sukanu Samiti,' he said. 'We should carry this mantle on our shoulders. We should protest in such a manner that the government has no option but to heed our demands,' he went on.

'We were saying the same thing, comrade,' I said.

He was happy to hear that. He said, 'Indrajit has proposed taking out a morcha from Nashik to Mumbai to raise farmers' issues. What are your thoughts on this?' He almost put forth a proposal.

'Comrade, it is almost like you read our minds,' I almost screamed in agreement.

Sunil Malusare and our activists from Nashik supported the idea entirely.

Comrade Gavit was thrilled.

'Come, let's go out for dinner and discuss it further at the dinner table.' He said.

We went to a nearby hotel where comrade Gavit started discussing the idea. He shared with us in detail what he had on his mind.

We told him that we were thinking on similar lines. 'Comrade, please discuss this with Dr Dhawale as soon as possible. You present your idea in tomorrow's session. We are sure that this Long March will be a grand success!' All of us were very excited about this idea and welcomed it wholeheartedly.

The next day, we met with at least 150 Kisan Sabha activists. Dr Dhawale shared national-level events, and I shared what had happened in Sukanu Samiti and the status of the farmers' protests in the state. Following this, comrade Gavit put up the proposal of the Long March for discussion.

All our party workers were eagerly waiting for some fruitful, direct action on the ground. The recent developments in the Sukanu Samiti had demoralized many. The idea of a Long March where thousand walked from Nashik to Mumbai was thrilling. Everybody welcomed comrade Gavit's proposal.

When farmers went on a strike, they had raised two critical demands. One of the loan waiver and the other of the minimum support price or the MSP. The agitation had overlooked the burning question of rights over forest land. Kisan Sabha had a powerful presence in Nashik, Thane, Palghar, and Adivasi areas of Ahmednagar district, and we knew that people were unhappy and there was growing anger about this issue. Along with this, farmers across the state were fighting for rights over lands belonging to temple trusts, grazing lands, or benami lands and for irrigation, food on ration, and pension. We needed to talk about these issues and the core demands for loan waivers and MSP. This would boost our strength. We discussed these issues in detail, and finally, the protest was announced. Dates for the march were declared. We wanted it to coincide with the budget session of the Assembly. The march was to leave Nashik on 6 March, and all the workers from various districts were instructed to reach the city by 11 am.

All of geared up. The decision to take out the Long March was announced on 18 February. We would reach home the next day, on 19, and the march would begin on the 6 March. We hardly had two weeks to prepare. It was a considerable challenge. But all the brave Kisan Sabha soldiers took it upon ourselves, and we sounded the bugle.

66

Kisan Sabha organized a Press Conference on 21 February in Mumbai to formally announce the Long March. Dr Dhawale, Indrajit Gavit, Irfan Sheikh, MLA Gavit, Kisan Gujar, Sunil

Malusare, and I were present. Reporters were present in good numbers as they had seen Kisan Sabha work during the farmers' strike. We had a good dialogue with the press but not much coverage the next day.

Thousands of farmers had planned to walk for seven days, covering a whopping 180 kilometres from Nashik to Mumbai. They were determined to gherao the Assembly.

Were they going to walk? Really?

No one was ready to believe and had refrained from giving the news.

Many thought that this would end in two days or we would end it, claiming no-go from the police. Many said that openly.

But we were determined. We held another press conference at Nashik. It was vital for us to reach out to the farmers across the state, and to do that, we wanted the mainstream media to discuss our march. So, we talked to the press on the 2 March. And we called for a meeting to finalize the distribution of work among our team and take stock of our preparations.

We have always had good support from the press in Nashik, and many were present at the press conference held after our meeting. Our proposed campaign was covered well in the district editions of many dailies. We were yet to reach a stage where we could promote the Long March across the state. People were still not confident that such a march could materialize. Kisan Sabha was preparing for it with all its might.

Our team of Indrajit Gavit, Irfan Sheikh, MLA Gavit, Kisan Gujar, Savaliram Pawar, Subhash Choudhary, Sunil Malusare, and Vijay Patil, along with hundreds of party workers, were visiting villages in Nashik district and preparing for the Long March. Dr Dhawale, Barkya Mangat, Mariam Dhawale, Radka Kalangada, and Ratan Budhar focused their energies on the Thane-Palghar district. Kisan Gujar and I participated in the Thane-Palghar district meeting. We then began with our regional gathering of people and activists from Ahmednagar. Aradhana Borhade, Dnyaneshwar Kakad, Eknath Mengal, Khandubaba, Lahu Joshi, Mathurabai Barde, Namdev Bhangare, Sadashiv Sabale, Sahebrao Ghode, Sarangdhar Tanpure, Shantaram Barde, Yadavrao Navale, Zubeida Maniyar, and numerous grassroots workers were putting in all their energy to mobilize people in the district. All the office-bearers from the state were working very hard to make the Long March a huge success.

V

67

March 6 2018. We reached CBS square in Nashik at around 10 am. Thousands of farmers were to gather here and start towards Mumbai, covering a distance of 180 kilometres on foot to present their demands to those in power. This was a historical event. We were standing under a tree on the right side. Two years back, on 29 March 2016 were had gathered at the same spot for the *Mahamukkam Satyagraha*, a mega sit-in organized by the Kisan Sabha. Around one lakh farmers had stayed put in this same square to voice their demands. It was a historical *mahamukkam*. That satyagraha was instrumental in bringing forth the demands for land entitlement, freedom from debt, MSP, pension for farmers and farm labourers, drought mitigation, irrigation, and crop insurance. And just after two years, we were standing at the same place for yet another agitation. So much had happened in the last two years. The strike by farmers, protests by the Sukanu Samiti . . . we had come so far!

People were trickling in, and CBS square was coming alive. Thousands of farmers were to gather here, not to sit in but march towards Mumbai. My thoughts were all over.

And, it began. The contingent from Ahmednagar was the first to arrive. Familiar faces, holding their bags alighting the vehicle, walked towards me. Sadashiv Sabale from Akole was a devoted activist. We had distributed red caps for all the marchers, and Sadashiv was responsible for the distribution. A man of small built, Sadashiv, was going to carry his own luggage and bags full of caps. But he was not complaining. He started his task with the Ahmednagar contingent, registering the names and keeping the sale records. Slowly, the red caps adorned the uncovered heads, and the red wave soon engulfed the CBS square.

The Nashik contingent arrived around 1 pm, and so did the farmers from Thane and Palghar. Kisan Sabha leaders and activists from across the state had come. By 3 pm, the square was full of people. Twenty-five thousand farmers arrived on the first day itself. The numbers were to rise in the coming days. We were looking at around forty thousand farmers reaching Mumbai.

The march was to begin after the initial dialogue. Without waiting for the mic and speakers, we began addressing the gathering with the megaphones. Ex-minister and senior leader from the PWP, Minakshitai Patil, was present to address the farmers. Around 4 pm, this vast contingent of farmers started walking. Everyone was wearing a red cap, and this had a dramatic effect. MLA Gavit, Dr D. L. Karad, and the Kisan Sabha office bearers were leading the March. All of us were thrilled. The air was filled with calls for *Chalo Mumbai*. We were on the verge of creating history.

All the state and district leaders of Kisan Sabha were going to walk with their fellow farmers for the next seven days. Manohar Mule from Shetmajoor Union, Nagpur, and Vinod Nikale from CITU, Thane-Palghar, also decided to walk along with us in solidarity.

The first stop was on the banks of Waldevi river on the Nashik-Mumbai highway. Indrajit Gavit, Irfan Sheikh, Kisan Gujar, Savaliram Pawar, Subhash Choudhari, and Sunil Malusare had each and everything planned well. Tankers for drinking water had arrived, and efforts were on to put up diesel-generator sets. Farmers were carrying enough grains to last for the next seven days. They also brought cooking fuel, all the ration, and cooks from their villages. On the first day, there was no need to cook as all the marchers had carried *bhakri* for lunch and dinner. They were instructed to do so.

We walked for 15-16 kilometres and reached our first destination point. It was pitch dark. We were going to spend the night a little inside from the highway. There was no light. It was a barren plot of land in the forest nearby. We asked everyone to gather near the open plot in front of one hotel to instruct them regarding the stay. The police had blocked traffic from one direction. It was safer to close a section of highway, at least a kilometre, and let the farmers use the road to sleep on. It was much safer than the forest plot as there was fear of snakes and scorpions. We requested the police to permit us to use the road, but they declined. We did not want to start a fight on the first day, so we agreed. After some initial instructions, we started walking towards the forest plot in the dark of the night. Thousands of farmers, women, children reached the ground. I was quite scared thinking of all the risks. And, we had made the plunge.

68

It was the break of day. The night had passed, and we were safe. The farmers were up quite early, all ready to start. The vehicle carrying the mic and speakers had reached as well. They wanted to walk as much as they could before noon. The march began much before the sunrise. Vehicles carrying food and the cooks went first to start the preparations for lunch. Each village had arranged one vehicle for this purpose through donations and contributions. And they had arranged for rice, dal, vegetables, oil, and other staples that would last for a week. Kisan Sabha had not provided any money for this. It was only through their contributions. They were carrying firewood and not just that, big rocks to set up the chulha (traditional earthen or brick stove). This was the wisdom of these folks. They had left their village fully prepared, from grain to the matchsticks, all under the able guidance of local leaders and wise farmers. Looking at their preparations, there was no stopping the Long March from reaching Mumbai.

We had decided to halt at Khambale near Igatpuri for lunch. The cooks had planned to keep rice and dal ready for the marchers. All those who did not have their own arrangement for food would also join others for lunch. Farmers kept marching towards Mumbai, unbothered with the heat and sweat on the hot tar road.

We stopped for lunch around 1.30-2 pm and had our meals under the blistering hot sun. Water was tepid, and we made do with it. We had planned to spend the night in the open ground of the Ghatandevi temple near Kasara ghat. Thousands of farmers were inching towards the campsite. The all-India Joint Secretary of Kisan Sabha, Vijoo Krishnan, arrived from Delhi the previous night and joined us on foot. Four megaphones and two speakers atop a vehicle played songs from the farmers' movement and slogans in between. The atmosphere was electrifying. The music and the energy made us forget our painful feet. I could only hear the beauty of the music and not the pain of my feet.

We almost didn't feel the pain anymore.

How could we feel the pain? We have to ignore it. The pain of selling our produce for a pittance and the daily loot. The pain caused by the total disregard, apathy and insult – of our plight from generation to generation – of wounds and abject poverty.

The life of a peasant is all but vain.

So be it.

We didn't bother about our feet anymore. We just kept marching.

The vehicles carrying food and cooks had reached the Ghatandevi temple ahead of us. It is a beautiful temple with a large open area covered with giant trees and climbers. All we could see in the darkness was open fire chulhas every few metres as we reached. The burning coals and fire had a magical effect, and the cool, soothing breeze made it truly beautiful. TV reporters were trying to capture these scenes in their cameras. Half an hour after we reached people were still entering the temple premise, where they sat in groups. More people had joined us for sure.

Soon, people sat down to eat along with their fellow villagers. Fresh hot food relieved them of fatigue. We gathered in the temple and began our short review meeting, and responsibilities were delegated. Prachi Hatiwalekar from the AIDWA had come from Thane and reached in the evening. There was a lot to do in Thane, including press conferences, arrangements for stay, necessary permission . . . the list was unending. Comrade Prachi was a big help. We were happy that things were right on track till now. As the meeting got over, we sat down for dinner.

As soon as the dinner got over, people started singing *Bohada*[6] songs. The sound of instruments filled the air. And soon, people were on their feet, moving to the rhythm of *Bohada* songs. The rhythm and the feet moving in tandem transported us to the beginning of our lives. The energy was captivating.

Words cannot express the energy, the mystic mood, the depth of the notes, and its organic connection. In unison with each other, we became one with our group, our tribe, fellow human beings, and humanity. We became one with nature and with the universe. No one was alone. The loneliness melted away in the eternity. The fear of being alone, the feeling of helplessness and doubt, was no longer there.

We were thoroughly engrossed, in unison with others. We could almost feel the mystic life force of our existence in this universe. Not one, but all.

Those notes made us forget ourselves, our world, and the entire universe per se. The notes healed us, made us forget our fatigue. The wellspring of happiness and the urge to live is not mired by the hardships of indigenous, harsh, and wild ways of life. Generations pass by, unhindered, unstopped. I felt it. Lived it.

[6] https://marathivishwakosh.org/17541/

The press had begun reporting the Long March. Social media was active. But we were yet to reach the conscience of people across the state. We had to do something more. The people of this country had to see the image of thousands of farmers descending the Kasara Ghat, marching towards Mumbai. That would genuinely show how unique this Long March is. If only we could capture in one frame the intimidating Sahyadri ranges of Kasara and, on its backdrop, thousands of resolute farmers descending the Ghats. We also needed to time it perfectly, just at the crack of dawn.

The Ghat was at a very close distance from our campsite. So, the march would not take much time to reach there. Six in the morning would be a perfect time. I shared my idea with Dr Dhawale. Ever supportive of new ideas, he gave his full backing. But some of our friends involved in the daily management were not for this as they felt that it is wise to leave early and cover as much distance as possible before the sunset. There is no need for a 'photo shoot', they said. They told me it is essential to reach in time for lunch to avoid wasting any time in the morning. For us, marchers descending Kasara ghat was a perfect opportunity to showcase the grandeur of this march, and thus we wanted to wait a little more. Considering the vast numbers, we could not convey the message to everybody, and finally, we began much earlier than our plan. I tried to capture the march going down the Kasara Ghat, but I could not. People had walked relatively fast and had gone ahead. Now, I was in search of another spot.

One side of the highway was closed for traffic for the march to descend the ghat safely. The section on the left was for vehicles, and we were descending from the right side. I had put caps and some other material in my car, with Digambar Kamble. Khandubaba was with him in the car, going down from the left side of the road. He is a very resourceful person in such times of crisis. I called him and told him: 'Khandubaba, I am walking in front of the march and am planning to take some photos on the next turn of the ghat. I can't reach it even if I walk very fast, and no way we can stop the entire march only for photos. I can see only one possibility. If you drive from the wrong side on our side of the road and pick me up, then we can go ahead and try something. We don't have much time. You can't descend the whole ghat and then come upwards. But please do something . . .'

Khandubaba has many tricks in his hat for such times. In his youth, he has travelled in this region. Many people came with their livestock for grazing in those days and stayed here in the summer months. Ghoti was the main market for livestock as well as farm produce. Farmers traversed this area for the market as well as for *urs* and other festivals. Later, during the communist movement, many active workers from our village and Akole taluka took refuge in these jungles. It was a safe place for the underground activists to meet and share messages. Khandubaba and folks from his generation have been familiar with this region since then. And, thus, he knows most of the roads, pathways, and secret routes in the hills.

'Is that it? Do not worry a bit,' he said and cut my call.

We passed the first turn. And the second turn, as well.

And, to my surprise, Khandubaba was coming up towards us! Impossible!

How could he come and reach us in such a short time?

Curious and jumping with joy, I got in the car. There is one route used by the bullock carts that connects the descending and ascending lanes of the ghat. Khandubaba knew this route. It was challenging to take my sedan car on this hilly road. Digambar was not very experienced. But Khandubaba took the risk and reached us through that route, driving up and down in my sedan car on that hilly bullock cart route.

It was Dr Dhawale and Khandubaba who shared my conviction about this. We reached the mid-section of the ghat and parked our car at the foothills of one range. Khnadubaba had taken an enormous risk to reach me, and now it was my turn to capitalize on that risk as well as I could. I had to climb the mountain range, crossing big anthills.

The instruments from our march played at a distance. The sound was coming closer and closer. I did not have much time and had to reach as high as possible. That would give me the right spot to cover the march descending from the ghat. It was a historic moment waiting to be clicked.

My eyes were fixed on a road circling the edges of these gigantic mountains rising high above the valley. I could hear the many sounds of nature as vehicular traffic was stopped. The instruments from the Long March were playing in the distance. I was standing on a higher cliff, balancing the tablet in my hand and eagerly waiting to capture that red thunder. And there they came. I could see some red figures turning at the edge.

The marching farmers resembles the forceful water flowing off the cliff. With red caps on their heads and red flags in hand, they walked with force. It was vast and bewildering. The vehicle carrying four speakers on the roof was descending slowly. People playing long *Pipani* danced behind the vehicle. The *pipani* was indeed a symbol of Adivasi culture. Behind them were our leaders, holding a long banner in their hand, leading the massive march. And behind them was a red sea of people, passing the twists and turns of the mighty Kasara.

I was at the right spot and had found the perfect angle for my shot. I wanted to make a 60-90 second clip, making it easy to upload and share on social media. Everything was right. The Long March was descending the Kasara playing the haunting Adivasi *dhun*. The clip was excellent. I climbed down the hill, almost jumping and crossed that massive sea of people and started walking as fast as I could.

I wanted to share my feat with Dr Dhawale. The grandeur and the thrill of the Long March can now reach all corners. I was hoping to get some network after we descended the ghat. All of us were exhausted with that walk and needed some rest. We stopped opposite a hotel on a water break. Farmers too relaxed a bit and had some water. And, my phone had a good network. The clip was ready. I shared it with almost 600 contacts. Watching that red sea of people descending the Kasara ghat with all their might was going to change the tide for sure.

70

We had walked almost 15 kilometres since morning. The pace had slowed down. The destination for lunch break was still two kilometres away. I got a call from Abhijit Kamble:

'Ajitbhaiyya, I have just received the footage from Kasara Ghat. Tell the name of the person who shot this. BBC won't publish it without a name. The clip is fantastic, and the Long March is truly something!'

'I have recorded the clip, but it is okay if you put in anybody else's name. That's a minor thing,' I said.

'I will put your name,' Abhijit ended the call, promising to call later. He sounded pretty upbeat.

Our friendship goes way back to Navoday Vidyalay. I was two years senior to him. Those were magical days. It is always such a pleasure to meet anyone from Navoday. All of us called our seniors Bhaiiya in school. And Abhijit still calls me Ajit Bhaiiya. He was a big help during the farmers' strike. At that time, he was with TV9, and now he was working with BBC in New Delhi. He was a massive help in circulating the Long March video.

Thousands of us walking on the blistering hot road finally reached our lunch site around 1.30 pm. People sat down for lunch in that scorching heat. Rice was served with dal with a very thin layer of oil and spices. I ate my rice and dal spiced just with chilli powder but it was no less flavoursome. The magic lies in the hands of the cook, they say.

After resting for some time, we were back on our feet, walking.

Dr Dhawale was with us, but MLA Gavit had to leave to attend the budget session of the Assembly. He planned to discuss with opposition parties and raise these issues in the house. Vijoo Krishnan left for Delhi the previous night. Irfan Sheikh, Kisan Gujar, and Sunil Malusare had gone ahead to look after the dinner preparations. Indrajit Gavit, Savaliram Pawar, Subhash Choudhari, Umesh Deshmukh, Vilas Babar, and I coordinated the movement of farmers and their contingents.

After lunch, the march had lost a bit of its steam. Some people were in a mood to relax, and some started to walk. Some were yet to finish their lunch. The vehicle leading from the front was still waiting in the ground. Those who began to walk were in no mood to wait for the vehicle to lead them. They had covered almost 4-5 kilometres before others joined in. Finally, we had to send the vehicle and get people to stop.

'Just go and reach our people. Park your vehicle right in the middle and request them to wait for others. We will gather everybody here and reach as soon as possible,' I told the driver. There we were, back on the road with remaining marchers. After a few kilometres, we could see the vehicle. We parked the water tanker next to it. The heat was blazing, and the marchers were not walking together. Just then, I received a call from an India TV reporter. He said: 'Your video clip has reached our Delhi office. And I have been told to cover the march. I will soon reach Shahapur. The national media has got the news and all of them want to cover the Long March. Where are you, right now?'

Wonderful!

All my efforts were paying off. I shared our location. Now, pushing myself once again, I started gathering all people together. We wanted the march to be organized. Khandubaba, Savaliram, Umesh, and Vilas were there to help and so were our activists from Ahmednagar. We wanted the same impact as that of the farmers descending the Kasara ghat.

And yet another call. P. Sainath, Sitaram Yechury, and some

renowned journalists from New Delhi had retweeted the video clip of the march in Kasara ghat. And as a result, many leaders, ideologues, reporters, journalists, and editors took cognizance of our march. The clip was also shared by hundreds of farmers' groups on Whatsapp and Facebook. It was a big hit on social media. And even in the mainstream media, the Long March was at the centre of discussion on many channels. It was getting much more coverage than the farmers' strike. All our helping hands in media were at work, I suppose. I was grateful for their support and marched ahead on our path. We were welcomed by more and more media persons. The regional Marathi media had stood by us since the beginning and now the national media was waking up to it. The government was in no position to ignore us anymore.

71

Tonight, we were staying in a large open ground near Kalamgaon just before Shahapur. Reporters outside Mumbai, like those from Pune, had arrived. Reporters from Marathi, Hindi, English news channels, and a few from other regional languages had reached the Khadi Phata. The open ground was not levelled, but it was clean and at some distance from forest or shrubs. Chulhas burned red in the moonlight. We met people from different villages and checked upon them for any complaints or discomfort. Irfan Sheikh called and said that we needed to start our meeting. He told me that the team from Nashik had gathered at the entrance of the ground and that they were waiting for me. I rushed there.

Most of the organizers were present and reviewed the events of the day. There were not many problems apart from, 'the distance between two stops (for lunch and night stay) is a bit longer. It is quite hard on elderly women and men,' some of us complained. We needed to review and select new stops and arrangements for the night stay, with less distance between the two stops. The entire timetable was up for changes now.

At the outset, we had travelled on this route and developed a thorough plan for lunch and night stops. We had checked out many options, but they were very few, considering we needed a place for more than forty thousand people. We had to ensure enough water supply for cooking, bathing, etc. We had to ensure that the place was away from shrubs and plant growth to avoid snakes and scorpions. The distance between the two stops could not be more than 15 to 20 kilometres. MLA Gavit, too had reviewed and approved these. But now, we needed to respond to the emerging issues and change a few locations. Kisan Gujar and Sunil Malusare were making the changes with due care. We had given them the freedom to take the final call after taking in all the suggestions. They needed to leave early in the morning to review and finalize a few places, mainly open grounds with enough water, and all this was to be done in coordination with the police. It was a crucial task with a lot of responsibility.

Till that day, no other government department barring the police had taken any cognizance of the march. Those in power had decided to disregard the Long March. They must have thought that we would walk for two-three days and return home exhausted. After our meeting, we were looking at the dinner arrangements. A few doctors working with the 108 Ambulance[7] came looking for me. They asked us if they could offer any help. I was speechless for a moment . . .

It was the third day of our march. Many had swollen feet with painful blisters. Many people hurt their feet badly, toenails had gotten pulled. Chappals were torn, and people walked barefoot, 'the skin of their feet peeling off'. Heavy bags on their head with clothes and bedding were causing strain on the back. Some could not bear the heat. This doctor friend was asking if we needed any help. What and how much could I tell him?

So, the bureaucracy had to pay heed, it seems.

---

[7] Government ambulance for emergency services reaching your doorstep.

The Long March had climbed down the ghat leaving behind hamlets and villages. We were on the plains near the city. They can no longer ignore us.

You have to come out in the open, on the battleground, my friend!

The hills and the valleys have heard you weep and cry from the time gone by.

All those rallies, protests, meetings and resolutions and the satyagraha were inside the villages, unseen and unheard.

Three lakh farmers hanged themselves, ending their lives from the trees on their farms. Out of sight of so many others.

But, the pain and agony of my cultivators, my farmers is far from over.

The countryside was being robbed of its life, its lifeforce, and cities were booming unconcerned and undeterred. With its self-centred, intellectual way of being, the urban middle class is almost of an autistic kind. The *maibaap sarkar* (the benevolent government) was equally unconcerned with the pain and distress in the rural areas. And the cities happy in their centuries-old slumber were praising the progress as and when they could. We had to come out of our village walls, on the ground, and end this dead to the world slumber. The *mahamukkam* at Nashik, the Farmers' strike, and the Long March did just that.

You have to come out in the open, on the battleground, my friend!

You screamed, in the hills and inside the village, far away from the cities. We have to knock at the walls of the city and pinch them where it hurts.

The Long March had come out in the open. The cities were in clear sight. The media was interested and active, almost like a modern-day third eye. How can anyone continue to disregard us?

Thank you, Long March! Thank you to the media.

The doctor with the 108 Ambulance wanted to help. Some of our fellows from the movement had provided medical help as the march began. Dr Samir Ahire had made available a fully equipped ambulance, and he was attending to the patients personally. The Maharashtra State Medical Representatives Association (MSMRA) had procured medicines through some doctors. But considering the huge number of marchers, any help was more than welcome. We shared what was required. Those doctors had received orders to provide medical aid within the area of their jurisdiction. He enquired a bit more before leaving left. He also said that the Divisional Officer was soon to meet us.

The number of marchers was growing. Thousands of farmers under the banner of All India Kisan Sabha had joined in. A contingent from Sangli came in the afternoon. The numbers from Ahmednagar, Palghar, Parbhani, and Thane had gone up. And most importantly, many farmers from Nashik had joined after watching the images of the march in Kasara Ghat. These events gave a big boost, big enough to make us forget our blistered and painful feet!

72

Day four began with a bang. Farmers were up and walking even before the crack of dawn. The media was covering the march minute to minute. We wanted to walk fast and cover as much distance as possible before noon. The lead vehicle had focus lights guiding us on the dark roads. We walked in tandem with the songs played on the speakers, falling in line, walking in unison, disciplined, and focused. Around 9 am, we crossed Shahapur. Many leaders from various political parties welcomed us, showed their support, and offered to help. We stopped for a break after covering a distance of 10-12 kilometres. And then, we were marching ahead.

The elderly women farmers were in excruciating pain. Many were walking barefoot as their chappals gave away. Their soles were blistered. As soon as the march stopped for a break, they would gather around an ambulance for some quick treatment for their wounds. The line of patients was longer each day. People waited to get their wounds cleaned and dressed in a bandage. Shekubai was one such farmer who got her wounds looked at every day but just didn't stop walking. It was painful to watch her, though.

The 66-years-old Shekubai from Varkheda in Dindori, didn't listen to anyone and came for the Long March. She walked from Nashik. Even when her chappals were torn – she walked. Covering her feet in cloth, she walked. She had to walk barefoot on the hot tar roads. Why? To save a tiny plot of land neither the blisters nor the pain could stop Shekubai.

Some reporters shared the photo of Shekubai's bleeding and wounded feet on social media. And that image made everyone feel the pain and sorrow of women farmers walking the Long March with their wounded and bloodied feet. There was anger. These photos uncovered the apathy and disregard by the state and showed their true and hideous faces to the world.

I simply could not take my mind off the image of our doctors pulling off the bloodied skin from Shekubai's feet. Not for a day, but for many days to come – that image of the blistered, bloodied feet of the woman farmer did not leave me.

How far has she walked? For how many days or months and years? Or for centuries, over generations? She has walked in silence, bearing the heavy burden of farming and agri'culture' on her shoulders. No complaints. And she has waited for someone to come and relieve them of the pain and dress her wounds.

She has walked this earth since the origin when her first ancestor put some seeds in the soil. Since then, she has been on her feet.

We are in debt of that first ancestor and Shekubai. The entire humanity is!

And us? What can be said of men . . .

The lesser said, the better.

Tonight, we would stay on the banks of the Bhatsa river. And for lunch, it was a large, open ground near Washind, just across the highway. We were about to reach the spot when I received a call.

'Hello Doctor saheb, this is the personal secretary of minister Eknath Shinde. Minister saheb has instructed me, and we are here to welcome the Long March. In the evening, he will come and visit you at the site. Shiv Sena Pramukh Shri Uddhav Thackeray has conveyed his support to the Long March. Shinde saheb is keen to arrange a meal for the farmers and has asked me to provide any other assistance.'

Getting a message from Eknath Shinde, support from Uddhav Thackeray and the request to help . . . was unexpected. We are followers of the communist ideology. And we have always been at loggerheads with Shiv Sena on the ideological front. But today, Shiv Sena supremo has welcomed our Long March. Something special indeed.

We had to welcome this support with a big heart. The ideological fights are never-ending. But at this moment, we have to be grateful for each and every kind of support that our cultivators receive from any quarter.

'We are thankful for the support from Uddhav Thackeray saheb and Eknath Shinde saheb, who has planned to come and meet us here. We are pleased to have you on our side. Kindly convey our gratitude to both these leaders. Regarding food for the marchers, I will have to discuss this with everyone as Kisan Sabha never takes such help from any political party. Farmers manage their food themselves in all our protests, which continues even in this Long March. But I will pass on your request to others and will get back in a while,' I said.

Vilas Babar and Umesh Deshmukh were with me, and Dr Dhawale was nearby. I got them together and conveyed the message. They all said that we should thank Shiv Sena for the support but humbly declined the offer to provide food. Eknath Shinde's secretary called in a while. I conveyed our decision – thanked him for the support, but we refused to accept food.

'Alright, no food. But don't say no to water. Let us at least do that for the farmers,' he appealed.

How could we say no to water? We agreed.

Support from Shiv Sena was an important event. They were in power and still supporting the Long March. This will push all other political parties besides BJP to come out and take cognizance of the march. This also allowed them to corner BJP to push farmers' demands. Wait and watch . . .

74

The sun was going down, and at around 5 pm, we reached the banks of the Bhatsa river. Today we stopped a bit early. There was abundant water for washing and bathing, and enough time to cook a good meal. That is why we decided to reach a little early. Kisan Gujar and Sunil Malusare had this planned well. It was a picturesque landscape. We saw hundreds of boxes with bottled water and a few Shiv Sena workers distributing these to the farmers as we walked towards the river.

I did not know that this beautiful river bed was this close to the highway. It was an excellent site to relax for a few days. We were crossing a bridge to reach our campsite. It was getting cold, and one could hear the water flow. Our marchers were happy swimming in the river bed, testing their skills. Some were bathing, others washing clothes. It looked as if an entire village had settled on the river bank hardly in an hour.

The sight after the sunset was beautiful beyond words. Heavenly, I would say. Under the open moonlit sky, people had set up their on-site kitchens, chulahs were lit, and the aroma of fresh *phodani* or a *bhagaar* had filled the air. Marching farmers found resting places on the unlevelled, uneven ground watched over by the giant trees.

Minister Eknath Shinde arrived. He did not act like a minister and came across as a simple, genuine person. Things looked fine.

We were sitting around our vehicle with speakers. Farmers joined us in a while. Shinde began his speech. He talked to the farmers and supported their demands. He reiterated his support for the Long March.

MLA Gavit was with us at the beginning of the march, and then he left for Mumbai for the Assembly session. Eknath Shinde called him and discussed with him. He also told us to contact him in case we needed any support.

We thanked him on behalf of the Kisan Sabha and urged him to go beyond this support – discuss and advocate – our issues in the cabinet. Comrade Gavit also reached our site late in the night.

Many news channels aired this gathering live on their channels. And many reporters stayed late in the night to cover this and talk to the farmers. Mandar Phanse from Mirror Now and a few other reporters talked to farmers late into the night. We invited them to join us for dinner. Along with rice and dal, we were lucky to have some vegetables on the menu. Today, our cooking teams got some extra time on their hand. All of us sat together for dinner – chatting and eating – I will never forget that meal.

75

Day 5 of the Long March. We started right before dawn. Bhatsa river had provided us with abundant water, and everything seemed rejuvenated. The mood was upbeat, and we could sense a new vigour in the march. Comrade Gavit had reached the previous night, and he would be with us. We walked fast, shouting slogans and singing songs. Mariam Dhawale and more than a thousand AIDWA activists joined us and walked with us in the morning.

Alka Dhupkar, a reporter from Maharashtra, was reporting from the ground. The march had picked up some speed, and suddenly, we heard some screams. Something was wrong, and people had gathered at a distance of around ten feet from us. We ran to the crowds and saw an elderly farmer sitting on the road – her feet and footwear were covered in blood. Her overgrown toenail got pulled as she walked.

She was in excruciating pain, but she didn't complain.

'Aai, come and sit in the vehicle.'

She picked up that nail and tied it back on the thumb with a tattered, unclean cloth. She refused to sit in the vehicle.

'Aai, you won't be able to walk now. There is an ambulance following us. Get your wound dressed. And travel in the vehicle,' we requested her again.

She did not budge and got up.

'I have to walk. I must.'

'Why?' asked Alka.

She got on her feet, balanced herself, and then she said, 'I walk so that my next generation does not have to come out on the road like this.'

Her eyes shined bright. Our eyes welled up.

Shame on this state!

The march resumed. All of us picked up some pace. It was just early morning, but I felt hot in the head. More than the blazing sun, it was this inner turmoil.

The march covered a distance of 13-14 kilometres and stopped for a short break. We entered one roadside hotel for a cup of tea. We saw comrade Gavit inside and went up to him. 'How to go forward with our demands?' I asked. Khandubaba and Umesh joined us. Comrade Gavit had a sombre look on his face. He was not his usual free and friendly self.

Umesh brought it up again. 'Comrade, we should discuss our demands and our strategy for the discussion with the government.

We should be prepared on which issues to focus and stress upon,' he urged him. Comrade Gavit was still very quiet.

'Comrade, we have to take up the issue of loan waivers. The situation is very grave. We have to pressure the state to take back all the terms and conditions. It is for us to carry on the work done by Sukanu Samiti. You had planned to take up our demands with some people in the Mantralaya. Did you meet anyone, and did you discuss these issues?' I asked.

'Yesterday, the CM called upon me. He wants to discuss these issues. But he made it clear that I should not invite you,' he told me.

'Farmers have joined the Long March for demanding forest rights and not a loan waiver or the MSP. Their main issue is of the forest land. If Ajit Navale is in a meeting, he will bring these issues up and disrupt the discussion,' Gavit shared. The CM has played another game.

Gavit had declined this suggestion, but I was extremely worried now and quite aghast at the CM's statement. This surely meant trouble. Was he trying to put the issues of loan waiver and MSP on the back burner? I could not finish that cup of tea or eat anything. That day I walked on that hot tar road carrying this heavy burden on my shoulders.

Let's not bring up issues of loan waiver and MSP . . .! Don't invite Ajit Navale on the delegation . . .!

Shame on this state!

76

We stopped for lunch on one large open ground near the highway in Bhiwandi taluka. The air was hot, but the ground grass cooled it a little bit. People from different villages had set up their tents on the ground. We sat down for lunch. Balasaheb Walunj, Chandrabhan Bhot, and Sandip Dhumal had come from Akole to visit us. Chandrabhan Bhot was much older than me, but we got along very well. All of us called him bhau. Whenever I was in Akole, he would often come to our hospital, and we spent the entire day chatting and discussing various issues. Balasaheb Walunj, Chandrabhan bhau, Heramb Kulkarni, Khandubaba, Shantaram Gaje, and many others would join us. Our conversations flowed freely – ranging from analysis of political happenings to social movements to local and global events to the recent books we'd read – these discussions were always deep and meaningful.

Bhau had a big circle of friends in Akole and the surrounding areas. Malunjkar mama (uncle) was one of his closest friends. He was senior to him, and all of us called lovingly called him mama, a resolute and proud person with a kind and compassionate heart. His was a big family, and four generations lived under one roof. Meeting him was always joyful. He was very passionate about the farmers' movement.

Bhau and mama were like Ram-Lakshman, and never left each other's side. Mama was diagnosed with some heart ailment. And, one day, he died in his sleep. His sudden death matched his proud and independent persona. He didn't suffer any pain. He looked as if he was fast asleep. After mama's passing, bhau was a changed person. He talked less. If we talked about mama, he would join us and speak as if he was okay, but his eyes showed he was hurting and in pain. It is not easy to lose someone! Slowly, bhau got over the loss and socialized with us. Such a fine person! He was a tremendous support. It was such a pleasure to see him walk towards us at the Long March. It is reassuring to have one's own people to support and encourage – a rarity in this self-centred world.

We sat down for lunch with bhau, Sandip, Balasaheb, and other comrades. Anil Autade, Rupendra Kale, and Yuvraj Jagtap worked with Raghunath Patil. They had brought with them homemade *bhakri, thecha,* and *pithala.*

'Doctor, don't mind what the senior leaders do. We are with all those fighting for the farmers,' said Autade. I was happy to hear that. I was feeling overwhelmed and motivated at the same time.

'We will keep at it, Anilrao,' I said.

What more could I say?

Everyone was back on the road after lunch. Bearing heat and harsh sun, we walked in tune with the protest songs: a kafila, a caravan of forty thousand people.

A caravan crossing the barren land and deserts, indeed.

The life of a farmer is nothing but a desert, and the oasis is usurped only by a handful.

Generation after generation . . .

Damn it!

77

The sun had set. We were still on the road. Avinash Jadhav from Maharashtra Navnirman Sena (MNS) reached us and said he wanted to convey a message from their party president, Raj Thackeray. He told me that Thackeray wished to speak with me and handed over his phone. Raj Thackeray was on the line. He welcomed all the farmers and said that we had his full support. I thanked him for that.

This was good.

Raj Thackeray supports the Long March. MNS workers all set to welcome the farmers in Mumbai! TV channels flashed the news.

The night stay was at the Anand Nagar Ground, Thane. ABP Majha had planned a live session from the ground, Prasanna Joshi was going to anchor the show. The preparations were in full swing.

The red storm of the farmers' army is all set to hit Mumbai! The stage was all set with banners with such slogans as the backdrop. Dr Dhawale, MLA Gavit, Mariam Dhawale, Umesh Deshmukh, Vilas Babar, and I were on the panel. The farmers were our audience. The programme went well. Since morning, many Marathi news channels such as TV9, Saam TV, IBN Lokmat, Zee 24 Tass had covered the march. And so did the Hindi and English media. Daily newspapers had published full-page stories and many social media channels circulated images from the Long March.

The entire state was thoroughly fascinated by the Long March.

Until very recently, the Sukanu Samiti had enthralled it fully. But where was it today?

No one saws off the branch that one sits on!

So be it.

Many people from nearby housing colonies poured in to show their support. They told us of their roots 'in the countryside' and shared fond memories. We felt connected and sensed their warmth. They live in cities but still belong to the village. It is very difficult to break ties.

78

So, the issue was that the CM did not want Ajit Navale in the meeting. It is as if the problems of loan waiver and MSP no longer exist. He wants to discuss all the other issues but not these critical demands.

They don't want Ajit Navale because he demands freedom from debt for thousands of farmers in the state. And he resists any attempt of exploitation which leads them to debt again and again. And he wants a fair price for their labour.

But is it only him? Is he the only one making such demands? Absolutely not! Thousands of wise and educated young farmers are demanding the same thing. When we have our produce, you loot us by intervening in the market, importing food grain, or bringing a ban on exports. You robbed our fields and harvests to build your cities and industry. You filled the coffers of the rich. But what did you do for the cultivators? You trapped them. You tied them to their farm. You dismantled and devastated our farm, our farming, and our countryside. Who are you to waive our loans? If not for this loot of our labour and our wages, we would have given you a loan.

Not just the CM but directors and chairpersons of various

state financial institutions create an adverse opinion about loan waivers. The chairperson of State Bank of India, the Governor of RBI, and the NABARD Chairman have given statements against the loan waivers since the farmers' strike. They claimed that such waivers are a misuse of taxpayers' money, it is bad for the fiscal discipline of banks, and it encourages borrowers to default.

We often believe that only those in business, jobs, or industry pay taxes. There is a strong belief that farmers do not pay taxes at all. The fact is that even if a farmer does not bear any direct taxation, they have to pay innumerable indirect forms of tax on all essential goods, various tools and equipment, and other inputs and services in farming. There are multiple kinds of taxes that have to be paid while selling one's produce. It is more of loot than waiver from taxes. But those in the seats of power don't want to understand the reality. It suits them not to.

Another question often asked by the opponents of loan waivers – why should the taxpayers pay for these waivers? Taxpayers pay their taxes for good governance and building infrastructure. They do not pay from their pockets for waiving someone else's loan. This seems like a sound argument. But one needs to understand that as people do not pay for waiving someone else's loan, they also do not want their money used to bring down produce prices. When prices of steel, cement, clothes, or medicines shoot up, the government does not intervene and import these goods using the taxpayers' money to regulate prices. But this is what the state does when it comes to regulating prices of the farm produce. The government intervenes, imports and regulates prices in the market, and for this, the taxpayers' money is used. And this move is justified in the garb of controlling inflation. Here, neither the issue of morality nor competition in the free market is raised. Nobody questions such misuse of taxes. These actions often devastate the farmer. But nobody cares. People question the government if it does not intervene and regulate or bring down the prices. Inflation is a good excuse, then. On the one hand, taxpayers' money is used to bring down prices of the farm produce which in a way denies the farmers their share of earning; then what is wrong if that same money is used to support a loan waiver that compensates this loot?

The second objection is that such waivers are damaging to the fiscal discipline of the banks. Agricultural loans are a fraction of what corporates borrow from the banks. Thus, the default amounts are quite less than the corporate sector. But banks do not send recovery teams to big business houses. Such unpaid loans are declared as non-productive assets (NPAs) and are written off. There is not much noise about this. There are hardly any debates on whether such bad loans should be written off using taxpayers' money or by banks that are government assets. Banks have secretly undertaken such transactions for many years.

This has resulted in doubling the NPAs in the last five years. At the end of 2015-16, the bad loans accounted for 6.95 lakh crores. By December 2016, unpaid loans and restructures amounts were almost 15 per cent of the total lending. Nobody talks about the fiscal discipline of the banks. On the contrary, the chief economic advisor of the country, Arvind Subramanian, was advocating waivers for such big defaulters. He considered this as necessary for managing the NPAs. There was no other option but a loan waiver for him, even though it might be seen as advocating corporate interest. He shared these views in a public speech at the Hormis Memorial Lecture organized by the Federal Bank.

The heads of the financial institutions and opponents of loan waivers often claimed that such a step results in a tendency to default. This was strange. It was an insult to the genuine and sincere effort of the farmers to pay back. Most of the farmers were stressed because they were not earning enough from farming, and in turn, they were unable to repay their loans. This was seen as an insult or failure, and this was a significant cause of distress among farmers. They were not distressed about the inability to repay. And many chose to end their lives because of this. And here, these policymakers were talking about the integrity of farmers. They were more concerned about fiscal prudence than the lives of the farmers. The same rule never applies to the big defaulters. We have never really heard of such big defaulters ending their lives because of their inability to repay. And the numbers show us that being a defaulter has become a norm in this class. Those heading the financial institutions never see this contradiction.

On this backdrop, we don't ask for the loan waiver as a favour, but we demand it as compensation for this age-old loot. We want long-term solutions and an impetus to rural employment. The development framework needs to be broadened. The farmers want their government to discuss these issues, and this Long March was an opportune moment for that. But was anyone bothered about their expectations?

Our concern was about being in power. We were bothered only about our timely salaries and the income under the table.

Nobody wants a debate.

Ajit Navale is frowned upon. Loan waiver and MSP are better not discussed.

I could not take my mind off this demand. I met Dr Dhawale as soon as the ABP Majha programme got over.

'Comrade, I think we need to sit down and have a unanimous position among ourselves,' I said.

Dr Dhawale called comrade Gavit, and Kisan Gujar contacted other office-bearers. Around 11.30 pm, we sat in one corner outside the ground. Gavit shared his conversation with CM. All the members unanimously rejected CM's suggestion of keeping me out of the delegation. We took up other issues such as which demands to push for, where to draw a line, and our strategy for the meeting. We also decided on who will raise which issue.

The meeting and the discussion went off quite well, but I was still quite upset. We got up at around 2 am. All the marchers were fast asleep. We had not had dinner, so we went out and searched for food. The street vendors only served bread and omelette or Chinese food.

I am a vegetarian. Always in the minority.

Shall I start eating meat? No, I shouldn't.

Another night without any food. It was 3 am when I lay down. But I could not sleep on an empty stomach and a troubled mind. We have to reach a decisive end on the issue of loan waivers.

79

It is 11 March today. The Long March is in its sixth day. The day started a bit late. All of us were exhausted so I got up a little late. People were reheating the leftover rice and others were preparing a fresh batch of dal and rice. We wanted to finish our breakfast by 8 am and then start the march. Bhai Jayant Patil, PWP (Shekapa) had arrived to welcome the march. The march was to begin after a formal gathering. The programme was midway when some reporters from the news channels approached me.

'We have heard that the CM has put a condition that he does not want you in the delegation. Is it true?' they asked. Journalists have their informers and 'sources' just everywhere, it seems.

I told them that it was true but I had full faith in the Kisan Sabha leaders and this was not going to be accepted. I also told them that it would not make any difference even if I was out of the delegation. Other leaders were equally accomplished, and they will press our demand for loan waivers and MSP. 'We won't back down till our demands are met,' I assured them. But the word was out, and the discussion around it was not going to die down. The news channels had got a piece of good news to run their shows on: 'The CM opposes Dr Ajit Navale's name in delegation!' How strange!

We left Anand Nagar around 11 am. The media was with us, and their number was increasing. Most of the national channels had live coverage of the march. We were back on our feet, under the harsh sun. Bhai Jayant Patil walked along with us. For the first five days, we were walking in forests or barren lands. But now we were in the city, surrounded by the urban crowds that watched us in awe. Many local leaders and their party workers came and greeted us on our way. They joined us as we walked. A day before, senior RPI leader Jogendra Kawade walked with us for an hour. Many others from INC, NCP, Shiv Sena and MNS came to meet us.

Almost all political parties, except the BJP had supported this Long March. They had endorsed the alternatives put forth by Kisan Sabha to tide over the agrarian crisis. We welcomed their support but the fact is that these same parties and their farm policies were at the root of the agrarian crisis. The INC and NCP during their long regime had propagated globalisation, liberalisation and privatisation and abandoned agriculture. They had left the farmers and their livelihoods at the mercy of the free market. And today, it was the ruling BJP and Shiv Sena that continued these policies with increased force and rigour. The alarming number of farmers' suicides were the result of these lethal policies.

Do they ever think of their own deeds when they support the Long March?

I don't think so.

Will they change their perspective and rethink their policies after this massive revolt?

I don't think so.

Anyway.

The images on the TV screen flashed every second. All of us were charged up with this boost. Around 1 pm, we stopped near Vikroli for a short break as we had had our lunch before the march. Many political parties and local mandals had made arrangements for water, sharbat, biscuits and other refreshments. After a while, we resumed our march. Soon, Aditya Thackeray approached us and reiterated Shiv Sena's support. And then, we learnt that minister Girish Mahajan was about to arrive and welcome the Long March. Kapil Patil, MLA from Lokbharati, and MLA Jitendra Awhad from NCP had already arrived.

The Long March had truly arrived!

How long will we shout and scream in the hills and forests? We have to come out and bang the city walls.

Except for BJP, almost all the prominent political parties supported the Long March. Politically, BJP was completely isolated and had lost its face among the farmers. The CM had sensed this. The fact that Girish Mahajan was here to meet us was a sign of that. He came and met us around 4 pm. He walked with the Long March and discussed a few things with comrade Gavit. He insisted that we should sit somewhere and talk to each other. There was a government office in the vicinity. Dr Dhawale and I went there to talk to him. Kapil Patil, Jitendra Awhad and Bhai Jayant Patil were present. They, too, were part of the discussion. Mahajan listened to our demands. Dr Dhawale and comrade Gavit stood their ground and said that the issue of loan waivers will be discussed in the meeting and the issue will be presented by none other than Dr Navale. They explained all the demands and expectations of the Long March. This discussion was more like briefing, and after this initial discussion, Mahajan was expected to report to the CM and then contact us. He kept pleading, 'Try and understand, we should resolve these issues through discussion'.

Ignoring us for six days had proven fatal. The red army had barged in. There was no way out than to sit down and discuss.

80

In the evening, the Long March reached Ramabai Ambedkar Nagar. It was an incredible sight. Thousands of people had gathered. Some had put up stalls distributing water, sharbat, biscuits and snacks. They welcomed us like none other. We reached the statue of Dr Babasaheb Ambedkar and decided to rest for a while.

All those who could liberate themselves from the shackles of rural life were here to welcome us all who are still caught in that trap. Around three generations back, these brothers and sisters left the dreadful rural life and turned to the city. They took shelter on the edges of this new land and survived doing whatever work that came their way. They survived and raised their young.

They had found their liberator, their muktidata.

We were still in search of one.

I did not want to get up from there, from the feet of that liberator.

Various leaders put garlands on Babasaheb's statue. The slogans of solidarity of Dalits and workers filled the air. Many leaders spoke. Mahendra Singh, member, Central Committee, CPI (M), Dr S.K. Rege, Member, State Committee, Shailesh Kamble, committee member, Mumbai, were running around since morning. All of them looked happy. The solidarity between farmers, farm labourers, Adivasi, Dalits and workers was heart-warming.

This should last, this unity among us. For now, and for good.

It should be a strong and tenacious front.

But this does not come to pass.

I heaved a sigh and got up. Everyone was up on their feet. The Long March had resumed.

Where to?

Come, let's go!

At each crossroad after Ramabai Nagar, we had the same experience. Thousands of kind and compassionate souls were out on the street to support the farmers. We were overwhelmed by this show of love and camaraderie. All of us were speechless.

Tonight, we were to stay at the Somaiya ground. TV9 had planned a live show straight from the ground. All the key leaders were on the panel. Nikhila Mhatre anchored the show. Dr Raju Waghmare from the INC was on the panel as well. K.K. Ragesh, a CPM MP from Kerala had arrived at the Somaiya ground. The farmers came in large numbers. The ground was full of people, filled beyond its capacity. We were witnessing a sea of people and their kindness and compassion. Our friends and family back at home were happy to see this support. They called and cheered. Everyone was happy. Our struggle had won Mumbai's heart.

Fantastic!

We came a long way today. The mood was exuberant. Activists from various organizations across the state had gathered at the Somaiya ground. Rohidas Dhumal, Anil Dethe of Bhumiputra Shetkari Sanghatana, Santosh Wadkar, Sainath Ghorpade of Kisan Sabha had reached around noon. And with them, they carried bhakri, pickle, thecha and dry pithala, a staple diet of Maharashtra's countryside.

Everybody was teeming with excitement. We were discussing some issues and we learnt that Raj Thackeray was about to arrive to support the Long March. And soon he reached the venue. We had built a stage at the entrance of the ground. Comrade Gavit welcomed him there and Thackeray in his peculiar style conversed with the farmers. He attacked the existing policies of the ruling government. Once his speech was over, he came and met us. We had a hearty conversation before he left.

Now, we had a serious issue to ponder over. Students appearing for their 10th board exams were writing their papers the next day.

The Long March was to head towards Azad Maidan. Forty thousand people were to walk the busy streets of Mumbai. A few errant drivers can bring the traffic to halt here and it takes hours to get it back on track. A massive rally of forty thousand people would run havoc. The impact was beyond our senses. The students would find it extremely difficult to reach their exam centres. We did not want them to suffer and let their efforts go down the drain. The city dwellers had supported the Long March with all their good wishes. Now we had to step up and show our solidarity and not harm their children's future.

What to do? We were in knots.

All of us were on the stage thinking of possible ways out. Our farmers had walked a very long distance and they were extremely tired. They could not even sit up and were almost falling asleep.

Option 1 - We spend the day here and leave for Azad Maidan the next evening.

Option 2 – We start after 12 pm.

Or if we start very early, around 3 am and reach by 10 am.

Or we leave right now, in the night.

We had to make sure that the roads were clear at least two hours before the exam starts.

These were our own children!

'Let the farmers take a call. We should leave it for them to decide,' said comrade Gavit.

He stood up, took the mic and explained the situation to everyone. He shared all possible alternatives and appealed to people to make a decision.

We were happily surprised to hear what people had to say.

'Let's finish dinner and leave for Azad Maidan. Getting up early looks difficult tonight. It is better that we leave late in the night,' said one marcher.

'Yes. We agree. Let's move now,' said many voices.

I was completely overwhelmed by this show of courage and compassion.

They truly considered these children as their own.

It was truly a sea of humanity.

People sat down to eat and finished their dinner quickly. Within an hour, the march was back on the road. We had walked a distance of 30-35 kilometres from Anand Nagar to Somaiya ground in the day. Everyone was extremely tired. But instead of resting for the night, they chose to walk another 15-20 kilometres towards Azad Maidan. We were just about to leave and a fleet of 30 buses entered Somaiya ground. The city police had arranged these. I am sure they too were humbled by the generosity of our farmers. They have witnessed many agitations that thrive only on a nuisance value, protests which block roads, disrupt traffic and cause trouble. But our farmers decided to walk another 20 kilometres even when they had walked the for the entire day, bearing that harsh heat.

The police were trying to help us by arranging the buses. 'Don't walk any further, we will drop you to Azad Maidan,' was their request. They tried to convince the farmers. Many farmers were truly exhausted and the elderly, in particular, were in a very bad shape. Some were sick and we too felt that they should take the bus. So, we decided not to stop the police. It was up to the farmers to decide.

We knew very well that they would not budge.

'We have walked all the way, dada . . . Why bother about a bus for this last leg?'

'Let's go,' farmers told each other.

My eyes welled. I wiped my tears, and head down, walked silently towards Azad Maidan. I wanted to cherish that moment, the men and women walking those extra miles to avoid any trouble for the children of this city.

81

The Long March walked another twenty kilometres and reached Azad Maidan in the wee hours of 12 March 2018. Many news channels across the country had covered this supreme act of humanity, in live coverage, all through the night.

Your children are our own!

Your troubles are our worries!

It is not easy, to be this, to be 'human'.

This selfless act of farmers earned them praise from many supporters and comrades across India. Support poured in from all quarters. Mumbaikars were truly impressed by this midnight march of the farmers. As thousands of them entered Azad Maidan, the city embraced them with an open heart. Many farm leaders often present urban dwellers as the true enemies of farmers. They should have been here to witness this solidarity between the two.

Mumbaikars had brought food in those early hours. Many mandals had brought huge pots of freshly cooked masale bhat.

No one was Hindu, Muslim, Sikh or Christian here. All of them stood together in support of the farmers. The religious boundaries ceased to exist.

Images of many farmers walking barefoot had gone viral on social media. Bleeding toes and blistered feet . . .

Mumbaikars had got sacks full of footwear for their barefoot brothers and sisters.

Shetkari Kamgar Paksha (PWP) had collected one lakh bhakris from villages in the Raigad district. These, along with dried fish had reached Azad Maidan.

This was a true celebration of the love and affection of people.

The feeling of not being alone, having everyone with you gives you a boost and relieves you of worries.

The countryside and the city were all out in the open to support the farmers. They went beyond caste or creed, religion or language, they stood firm behind the Long March. All political parties came out in support. People were with us.

The only exception was the BJP!

The only one!

82

Around 10 am, we received a message from the government inviting us for a discussion. The Kisan Sabha had sent a list of delegates which included Dr Ajit Navale, Dr Ashok Dhawale, Barkya Mangat, Indrajit Gavit, Irfan Sheikh, MLA J.P. Gavit, Kisan Gujar, former MLA Narsayya Adam, Radka Kalangada, Ratan Budhar, Savaliram Pawar, Siddhappa Kalshetti, Subhash Choudhari, Sunil Malusare, Umesh Deshmukh, and Vilas Babar. The delegation did not follow any terms or conditions from the government. Around forty thousand farmers were present in Azad Maidan. We got their nod and headed towards the Legislative Assembly.

At the meeting room in the Vidhan Bhavan, CM Devendra

Fadnavis, Chandrakant Patil, Eknath Shinde, Girish Mahajan, Pandurang Fundkar, Subhash Deshmukh, and Vishnu Sawra were ready for the discussion. All the chief secretaries, secretaries and officials were present as well. The leader of opposition Radhakrishna Vikhe-Patil, Dhananjay Munde, former deputy CM Ajit Pawar and NCP leader Sunil Tatkare were present, too. Bhai Jayant Patil and Kapil Patil were always on our side and they too were part of the meeting.

The CM had a closed-door meeting with the few of us and then we had an open discussion with the leaders of the opposition. The meeting went on for more than three hours and the government had to agree upon many of our demands.

Adivasi farmers had participated in huge numbers in the Long March. The issue of entitlement of forest land to the Adivasi cultivators has been pending for many years. The union government had passed the Forest Rights Act because of the pressure from the Left parties. But, millions of Adivasi farmers were still awaiting their rightful ownership of the forest land. We had decided to focus on this issue over others. We had requested that the issue of forest land be taken up for discussion first. Surprisingly, the CM was keen to begin with the loan waiver.

'I am sure other issues will have a positive outcome. But in the end, if we disagree on the issue of the loan waivers, then the entire effort will go down the drain. So, let us first talk about the loan waiver,' said the CM.

'No discussion on loan waiver. . .! Ajit Navale should not be in the delegation. . .!' The CM had put these conditions not more than 48 hours back. Those were ringing in my ears. The Long March had made such a huge impact.

Adam Mastar is an expert in such discussions. He has a lifetime of experience in such matters. So, we expected him to initiate the talks. And, he did. He asked me to present our demands regarding the loan waiver. 'Comrade, we demand that the farmers should be completely freed of debt,' I said.

'Ajitrao, you are right. Your fight for total freedom from debt is on. But look at this as a step towards that goal and suggest how we can modify the existing scheme for the loan waiver. Once we fulfil that, we will move towards the next step. Right now, tell us what changes you want in the current scheme,' the CM responded. He was still very much non-committal on the issue of the total karjamukti – freedom from debt.

'We will keep fighting for that goal. The government is on the back foot due to the march. Let's use that and get them to remove the problematic terms and conditions in the existing scheme,' Dr Dhawale whispered in my ears. He felt that it is wise to get the government to accept our demands and guarantee some action. It should not be that the meeting ends in a deadlock and we return empty-handed. After this humungous effort of the Long March, we should not lose our case because of any rigidity on our part. There was no other way than to take this route.

As the outcome of the farmers' strike, around 35.51 lakh farmers in the state had received some amount in their bank account under the loan waiver scheme. But millions of farmers were unable to access these benefits because of the terms and conditions put by the government. We had a golden opportunity to get these removed. Farmers who had taken loans during 2001-2009 were not eligible for the scheme. The scheme Agricultural Debt Waiver and Debt Relief scheme announced in 2008 had put the condition of the size of landholding, due to which millions of farmers were still out of its net.

The recent loan waiver had announced that the state will waive off women's loans on a priority basis. The announcement sounds nice to hear but there was a big catch. Only one person of a family is eligible to get the benefit of a loan waiver and thus small loan amounts on women's names were waived off. Men had a larger loan amount which was not considered for a waiver. The decision to extend the benefit for only one member too was detrimental.

The scheme did not waive off loans taken for Emu rearing, or construction of Polyhouse using Shade net. The cut-off date was 30 June 2016. Farmers who had accessed loans in 2017 were excluded so we wanted an extension of the cut-off date.

Numerous farmers failed to apply for the scheme because the entire process was online topped with such unjust conditions. The deadline had to be extended to allow such farmers to apply.

We demanded that all these preconditions be removed and all farmers are allowed to access the scheme. This would have put a huge financial burden on the state coffers so the officials were reluctant to remove these conditions. They tried their best to raise several issues that will divert the discussion and stall the decision. But the pressure of the Long March was so high that the government had no other option but to change its position.

In the end, after neck and neck negotiations, the government acceded to most of our demands. It was agreed that instead of a family as one unit, each bank account holder will be counted individually. Those who had accessed loans during 2001-2009 would be considered for the scheme. So the loan waiver was effective from 2001-2016. It was agreed that after some data analysis, the scheme would be extended till 2017 with some changes to include farmers who had taken loans till 30 June 2017. Those engaged in Emu rearing and the owners of poly houses and shade net structures were included in the scheme. The deadline for application was extended. This paved the way for millions of farmers to access the loan waiver. We had taken a bold step towards complete freedom from debt.

There was a serious discussion on the issues with the implementation of the Forest Rights Act. The Act came into force in 2006 but farmers cultivating forest lands were still awaiting their entitlement. A total of 3,50,908 claims were filed but due to the flaws in its implementation, a whopping 2,72,675 claims were rejected. And all these and more were still stuck in the appeal process. Many claims were filed in the government offices but are untraceable now. The farmers are extremely agitated about this.

And the government had to pay heed to that anger. In the meeting, they had to promise that all the claims would be processed in the next six months and the forest lands will be transferred to the cultivators.

Now we brought up another very important demand – the implementation of the Swaminathan Commission report. The government promised that it will pursue this matter with the union government. After the farmers' strike, the government was compelled to form the state commission for agricultural cost price. Besides the appointment of the chairperson, the commission was almost defunct. We demanded that all three positions should be filled and the commission should be made fully functional. The government agreed to that. The new Sugarcane Price Control Committee was not yet formed which was complicating the issue of price. We pushed for the formation of such a committee. These demands need to be fulfilled as these were crucial for ensuring a fair price for farm produce.

Many other demands were discussed and the government agreed to hold meetings and resolve these issues at the earliest. These include increased amounts for the beneficiaries under Niradhar yojana, resolving issues around ration cards, compensation for farmers affected by pink worm infestation as well the hailstorm, diverting water from westerly flowing rivers to drought-prone regions, land entitlements to tillers of different kinds of lands such those owned by temple trusts, those under government control due to non-payment of revenue, as well as lands used in rice cultivation, rabbing, etc.; regularisation of houses constructed on community grazing grounds and milk rates.

The main focus of the Long March was on loan waiver, MSP that gives at least 50 per cent above the cost of production, and the right to cultivate government/forest lands. Along with this, we also brought to the fore the very important issue of irrigation for agriculture. The water from westerly rivers including Naar-paar, Damanganga, Wagh and Pinjal flows into the Arabian sea.

We demanded that this water should be diverted and used for irrigation in the state. We stressed the need for strengthening the legal aspects around water. The equitable distribution of available water in the state is a very complex issue. Many projects (in water conservation and irrigation) are incomplete, the state of canals is almost beyond repairs. This apathy and neglect of infrastructure is an important cause of droughts in the state. We were trying to bring these issues to the fore, more so because of the frequent droughts faced by the farmers. The government had to gear up and pay serious attention to these issues.

The Long March fought hard for its demands regarding an increase in the pension amounts for widows, the elderly, the destitute and the disabled. We stood firm on our demands about employment guarantee schemes, PDS, health and drought mitigation. We spoke about the problems faced by farm widows. The Long March did not limit itself only to a mainstream farmer. Our demands reflected an overall crisis in the countryside. We compelled the government to consider Adivasis as farmers. We built bridges and got other farm unions and farmers on our side. If we want to strike at the roots of this crisis, there is no other way than to unite. The Long March was a sign that the peasants' movement had turned a new leaf.

We have to be watchful about the implementation of the decisions. We have very often seen that demands are met, but the decisions do not come into force. Considering this past experience of our movements, we also put forth some conditions. We wanted the decisions in writing along with a time-bound action plan for the implementation of these decisions and the formation of joint committees for monitoring the progress. We also wanted the CM to table the approved statement of demands on the floor of the house. And we wanted a minimum of three ministers to come to Azad Maidan and promise the farmers that these demands will be acted upon. The government had to agree to these conditions on the backdrop of wider support for the Long March.

We got the government nod to our demands in writing, signed by the Chief Secretary of the state. The CM shared the decision on the floor of the house and announced a time-bound plan of action. Chandrakant Patil, Girish Mahajan, and Eknath Shinde came to Azad Maidan and promised the farmers that their demands were met and the decisions would be implemented soon. The farmers were resting under a large pandal and many stalwarts and leaders including Comrade Sitaram Yechury, the General Secretary of CPI (M); Narsayya Adam, the state secretary; Bhai Jayant Patil, Chief Secretary of PWP (Shekapa); Kapil Patil, Lokbharati; veteran journalist P. Sainath; Aamra Ram, the former general secretary and a powerful leader of Kisan Sabha from Rajasthan; K.K. Ragesh and Vijoo Krishnan, joint secretaries of the central committee; Mariam Dhawale, all India general secretary of AIDWA; Sudha Sundaraman, vice-president of AIDWA; Dr D.L. Karad, All India deputy chairman of CITU, were present on the stage. Dr Ashok Dhawale, MLA J.P. Gavit, and I shared the finer details of the approved demands. All the national news channels covered this programme live along with press coverage by many reporters.

The Long March culminated with this historical *sabha*. The farmers' movement took a very bold step with this march. All the farmers walking barefoot on those blistering hot roads had won their battle.

83

The week-long journey was over. All the fellow farmers would now leave for their homes. They were in a hurry to go back. I did not want to leave this place. I was weighed down with emotions.

When will we meet again?

I was nervous and longed to be with everyone again.

Brahma Chatte was a great support during the strike and also in the Long March. He had come to visit us at Azad Maidan. Many friends and reporters had gathered. ABP Majha was doing a one-hour live show on the outcomes of the Long March. Khandubaba, Vilas Babar, and senior journalist Abhay Deshpande were on the panel with me. Chairman of the CACP, Pasha Patel was to participate in the programme. Using that excuse, I kept roaming around the venue for some more time.

The Long March had achieved a huge feat. The government was compelled to agree to almost all the demands. The significance of the crisis in farming was now for everyone to see. But we had just won a battle, our fight for ending the loot was not over yet. The fight for freedom from debt was not going to end anytime soon. This was a small battle that we had won. The fight for dignity for the farmer, for the soil and farming, is a long-drawn battle. We have to continue our struggle based on justice and humanity. We can achieve a real victory only through a pan-India protest that can push for a turnaround in policy.

We have to fight a long battle.

We have to walk many more miles.

And continue to the Long March with this army of farmers.

Till we reach that abode that we dream of.

This feeling rose from deep down.

I kept wandering in the ground telling myself 'Keep walking... stop nowhere'.

I thought of many events in these recent years. The Puntamba resolution. Farmers' strike. The traitors and the formation of Sukanu Samiti. Maharashtra strike. The state-wide rallies and the Long March.

All these events inspired us and showed us what can be achieved through unity and solidarity among farmers. These will motivate our future generations to fight for their rights.

The march brought home a message that we can fight and we can challenge the regime.

The state may go back on their word, we never know. It might just do away with all that we earned through our protests.

But no one can dare take away the confidence of the young farmers.

The confidence to fight injustice.

To stand firm against the loot and exploitation.

To build bridges that forge friendships and human bonding.

And, the confidence to follow our dreams!

No one can dare take away this breath of life and conviction from these youngsters. Never.

Afterword:
The Kisan Movement in Maharashtra

Ashok Dhawale

Maharashtra is among the states that have a long and glorious legacy of the Kisan movement, and a rich history of peasant and tribal struggles against feudalism. The peasantry of Maharashtra was also in the forefront of the struggle for independence against British imperialism. Thousands of peasants were martyred in all these valiant struggles.

KING OF THE PEASANTRY

The history of peasant revolts in Maharashtra can be traced back to Chhatrapati Shivaji (1630-1680), who led a number of victorious battles against the oppressive Mughal rule of Aurangzeb. Their highlight was guerrilla warfare. It was the peasantry of Maharashtra that was the main force in these battles. Under his rule, Shivaji took several measures that benefited the peasantry, and these have been recounted in Govind Pansare's iconic book *Who Was Shivaji?*, and Mahatma Jotirao Phule much later hailed Shivaji as 'the King of the Peasantry'. It is for this reason – his remarkably pro-peasant rule – that Shivaji, alone among kings, is revered by the people of Maharashtra even after nearly 400 years.

There was nothing communal in the confrontation between Shivaji and Aurangzeb. All evidence in fact points to the contrary. The best example is the completely secular letter written by Shivaji to Aurangzeb when he imposed the hated Jizya tax on non-Muslims. Moreover, many of Shivaji's key military and administrative officials were Muslims.

EARLY PEASANT REVOLTS AGAINST BRITISH RULE

Early peasant revolts against British rule began. From 1826, the peasants of Pune district led uprisings which forced the British authorities to cede to them land holdings for low revenue charges. In 1844, Kolhapur and Sawantwadi witnessed a large-scale peasant revolt provoked by the British decision to increase land revenue in order to pay tribute to the princes. In 1848, the Rohillas of Nagpur took up arms. Around the same time, the peasants of Khandesh region rose up in protest against the land settlement which resulted in the increase of land tax. In protest against the British take-over of jungles and their effort to evict Adivasis from forests, there were determined struggles led by the Bhil, Mahadev Koli, Ramoshi, and other Adivasi tribes. Great Adivasi peasant leaders Umaji Naik, Raghoji Bhangre, and Baburao Shedmake valiantly fought the British and were hanged.

The peasantry of Maharashtra played an important role in the First War of Indian Independence in 1857.Among those who led the revolt were renowned figures like Nana Sahib Peshwa, Tatya Tope, and, of course, Rani Lakshmibai of Jhansi. All of them hailed from Maharashtra. Rani Lakshmibai's maiden name was Manikarnika Tambe, and she was the daughter of Moropant and Bhagirathi Tambe, whose native village was Parola in the Jalgaon district of Maharashtra. Along with these leaders, the peasantry also fought and died.

THE INFLUENCE OF MAHATMA JOTIRAO PHULE

One of the most radical social reformers of Maharashtra, and indeed of India, in the nineteenth century, Mahatma Jotirao Phule (1827-1890), was a great champion of the peasantry and he bitterly attacked both landlordism and caste oppression. His books *Shetkaryacha Asud* (*Whipcord of the Cultivator*) and *Gulamgiri* (*Slavery*) remain classics. The Satyashodhak Samaj that he founded had a major impact in the state.

Phule's influence was an important factor that inspired the peasantry to fight against landlords and money-lenders. In the famous Deccan Riots of 1875, the drought-hit peasants of Pune and Ahmednagar districts barged into the houses of rapacious money-lenders, ransacked all papers related to peasant debt and publicly burnt them on the streets in order to destroy all evidence. Due to this uprising, in 1879 the British Government was forced to enact the Deccan Agricultural Debt Relief Act. The Ramoshi rebellion, led by the legendary leader Vasudev Balwant Phadke around the same time, was eventually crushed by the British, and Phadke was sent to jail in Aden, where he died in a hunger strike.

WORKING CLASS JOINS THE STRUGGLE

Peasant struggles in Maharashtra on various issues continued in the first part of the twentieth century. They were now joined by struggles of the working class.

Narayan Meghaji Lokhande is credited with being the father of the trade union movement in India. He was a close follower of Mahatma Jotirao Phule. Around 1880, he founded the Bombay Mill Hands Association, which fought for and won some basic demands of the textile workers. He also took courageous initiatives on caste and communal issues.

In July 1908, the working class of Mumbai went on a six day strike, in protest against the court judgement sentencing freedom fighter 'Lokmanya' Bal Gangadhar Tilak to six years of imprisonment. The strike was accompanied by street fights between workers and the police and military of the British rulers. Lenin wrote about this strike, 'The Indian proletariat has already matured sufficiently to wage a mass struggle, class conscious and political.' The foundation conference of the All India Trade Union Congress (AITUC), the first trade union federation in India, took place in Mumbai on 31 October 1920. Renowned freedom fighter Lala Lajpat Rai was elected its first president.

In the 1920s, massive strikes and other militant struggles of the textile workers of Mumbai were spearheaded under the Red Flag of the famous Girni Kamgar Union (GKU) which was led by the Communist Party. One of the most memorable of these strikes was the six-month strike of textile workers in 1928. It was as a result of these bitter class struggles that the working class of Mumbai and Maharashtra won several of its rights and demands. Among the legendary first-generation leaders of these working-class struggles were B.T. Ranadive, S.A. Dange, S.S. Mirajkar and others. From Mumbai, these struggles spread to other textile mill centres in districts like Thane, Solapur, Dhule, Jalgaon, Nagpur, and so on.

Two cardinal features of these Communist-led working-class struggles were that they mobilised workers in the freedom struggle against the British, and they also championed the cause of secularism and working-class unity against the reactionary forces of communalism.

In 1930, the working class of Solapur rose up in revolt against British rule. They ousted the British rulers and took control of the administration of Solapur city. This became known as the Solapur Commune. The British clamped down and imposed a most draconian Martial Law. There was terrible repression. Four leaders of this struggle – Jagannath Shinde, Mallappa Dhanshetty, Qurban Husain, and Shrikisan Sarda – were hanged on 12 January 1931. On 23 March 1931, the British hanged three other illustrious and revolutionary martyrs – Bhagat Singh, Rajguru, and Sukhdev. Of these, Shivram Hari Rajguru hailed from a peasant family of Khed in Pune district of Maharashtra. Khed was later renamed as Rajgurunagar.

DR AMBEDKAR'S STRUGGLES
AGAINST CASTE AND LANDLORDISM

In the historic struggles against caste and landlordism that were led by Dr Babasaheb Ambedkar in the 1920s and 1930s, Ramchandra Babaji More and Shamrao Parulekar were two prominent leaders who participated. Both of them later joined the Communist Party. R.B. More was the main organizer of the famous Chowdar Lake Satyagraha at Mahad in Raigad district on 20 March 1927, which was led by Dr Ambedkar. It demanded the basic right of Dalits to draw water from public water bodies. R.B. More also took a leading part in the other historic event of Dr Ambedkar's public burning of the hated Brahminical text targeting women and shudras, the Manusmriti, again at Mahad on 25 December 1927.

Dr Babasaheb Ambedkar and Shamrao Parulekar led a huge 8,000-strong peasant demonstration on the Mumbai Assembly in 1938 against the *khoti* system of landlordism that was then prevalent in the Konkan region. Remarkably, the peasants had all come to Mumbai by boat from the then Ratnagiri district of Konkan region.

SECOND CONFERENCE OF THE AIKS HELD IN MAHARASHTRA

The All India Kisan Sabha (AIKS) was formed at its foundation conference at Lucknow on 11 April 1936. Some delegates from Maharashtra attended it. The second conference of the AIKS was held at Faizpur in the Jalgaon district of Maharashtra on 25-26 December 25-26, 1936. M.A. Rasul, in his detailed work, A

History of the All India Kisan Sabha, has recorded that, 'About 500 kisan marchers led by V.M. Bhuskute and J. Bukhari started from Manmad on 12 December and marched over a 200-mile trek and reached Tilaknagar, Faizpur at noon on 25 December carrying the Red Flag and shouting Kisan slogans. On arrival there they were received by Jawaharlal Nehru (Congress president), Shankar Rao Deo (Congress Reception Committee chairman), M.N. Roy, Maniben Mulji, Narendra Dev, besides Kisan leaders like Swamiji, Ranga, Yagnik, Jaiprakash Narayan, Bankim Mukherji and Shibnath Banerji, also S.A. Dange, M.R. Masani, Yusuf Meherali and other Congress, Kisan and labour leaders.'

Peasant struggles on various issues intensified in the mid-1930s in Thane, Nashik, Ahmednagar and other districts. The AIKS had chosen Shamrao Parulekar to be its organizer in Maharashtra. In 1942, after their release from a two-year British jail term for leading the anti-war campaign, Shamrao and Godavari Parulekar began work in the AIKS in right earnest. In 1943-44, the Kisan Sabha was started by them in the Kalyan, Murbad and Shahapur tehsils of Thane district. Shamrao and Godavari met P. Sundarayya and M. Basavapunnaiah, the future leaders of the historic Telangana armed peasant struggle, with whom they continued to have very close relations throughout their lives.

AIKS FOUNDATION CONFERENCE IN MAHARASHTRA

The foundation conference of the Maharashtra Rajya Kisan Sabha was held on 7 January 1945 at Titwala in Thane district. Godavari Parulekar has recorded that she, along with other activists, covered over 700 villages on foot and addressed 160 public meetings for this conference. More than 7,000 poor and middle peasants and agricultural workers from several districts attended this first state conference of the Kisan Sabha. The conference elected a 33-member state Kisan Council. Buwa Nawale from Akole tehsil of Ahmednagar district was elected the first president, Shamrao

Parulekar the first general secretary and Godavari Parulekar the first joint secretary of the Maharashtra Rajya Kisan Sabha.

HISTORIC WARLI ADIVASI REVOLT

It was this conference that sparked the historic Warli Adivasi Revolt led by the Kisan Sabha in Thane district. This revolt began on May 23, 1945 and continued for over two years. It abolished all forms of slavery and bonded labour, increased wages of agricultural labourers and succeeded to an extent in giving land to the tiller. This struggle is analyzed in Shamrao Parulekar's book *Revolt of the Warlis*, and Godavari Parulekar's book *Adivasis Revolt*.

The Adivasi Revolt gave its first five martyrs on 10 October 1945, when the British police, who were in league with a plot hatched by the landlord lobby, fired mercilessly on a peaceful gathering of over 30,000 Adivasis at Talwada, near the Talasari tehsil of Thane district. Comrade Jethya Gangad was among those who were killed in this state repression. There have been a total of 61 martyrs of the Communist Party and the Kisan Sabha in Thane-Palghar district since 1945 – victims of successive British, Congress, and BJP regimes, and three martyrs in Nashik district. Most of them have been tribals.

The foundation of the Maharashtra Rajya Kisan Sabha and the Warli Adivasi Revolt were the culmination of the anti-imperialist and anti-feudal struggle waged by Shamrao and Godavari Parulekar in the pre-independence era.

SATARA PARALLEL GOVERNMENT AGAINST BRITISH RULE

From 1943 to 1946, in another historic occurrence, British rule was overthrown for three and a half years and a Parallel Government (Prati Sarkar) was established in Satara and Sangli districts of Western Maharashtra. This was an armed offshoot of the 1942 Quit India Movement. It could be sustained for so long only due to the full support of the peasantry.

This magnificent revolt was led by 'Krantisinha' Nana Patil, who later joined the Communist Party and was elected AIKS National President in the 13ᵗʰ AIKS Conference at Dahanu in Thane district in May 1955. Nana Patil was later elected twice to parliament, from Satara in 1957 and from Beed in 1967. Among the other distinguished leaders of the Satara Parallel Government were G.D. Lad, Nagnath Naikwadi, Captain Rambhau Lad, and many others.

INDEPENDENCE AND THE LIBERATION OF DADRA AND NAGARHAVELI

On 15 August 1947, independence dawned over India at last. But on that day, over 600 Adivasis from Thane district owing allegiance to the red flag of the Communist Party and the Kisan Sabha woke up to freedom in jails, as did thousands of other Communists all across the country. The most famous among them was, of course, another legendary leader of the Indian people – A.K. Gopalan, who was to lead the AIKS as its National President and would also be elected to parliament for over two decades.

The liberation of large parts of Dadra and Nagar Haveli from Portuguese rule from 24 July to 3 August 1954, under the armed leadership of the Communist Party and the Kisan Sabha in Thane district, was a major event. This struggle was directly led by Shamrao and Godavari Parulekar. L.B. Dhangar and hundreds of Adivasi comrades participated in this struggle.

The holding of the 13th National Conference of the AIKS at Dahanu in Thane district from 19-22 May 1955, braving all kinds of repression and obstacles by the government, was another significant event in the history of the Kisan movement in Maharashtra. Towering leaders of the AIKS – such as A.K. Gopalan,

B. Srinivas Rao, Bankim Mukherjee, Dasarath Deb, E.M.S. Namboodiripad, Hare Krishna Konar, Harkishan Singh Surjeet, Jagjit Singh Lyallpuri, M.A. Rasul, N. Prasada Rao, P. Sundarayya, and others – attended the conference which was accompanied by a massive rally. Shamrao and Godavari Parulekar were the moving spirits behind this conference, in which 'Krantisinha' Nana Patil was elected as AIKS President.

Another great leader from Maharashtra, Godavari Parulekar, would also be elected National President of the AIKS at its 25th Conference at Patna in 1986. This was its Golden Jubilee session. She is the only woman to have held the post so far. In earlier times, Shamrao Parulekar had also been an AIKS central office-bearer for many years.

GLORIOUS SAMYUKTA MAHARASHTRA MOVEMENT

In the 1950s, democratic movements for the formation of linguistic states began in many parts. The ruling Congress Party went back on its pre-independence pledge to form such states. This was the reason for the movements like Aikya Keralam, Vishal Andhra, Samyukta Maharashtra and Maha Gujarat that swept these states in the decade of the 1950s.

The Samyukta Maharashtra movement, from 1955 to 1960, was led by the Samyukta Maharashtra Samiti, which comprised four main parties – the Communist Party of India (CPI), the Praja Samajwadi Party (PSP), the Peasants and Workers Party (PWP) and the Republican Party of India (RPI). The movement engulfed the state, with the peasantry and working class both joining it in huge numbers. In the massive repression that followed, 106 people were martyred in police firing. Most of them were from the working class in Mumbai and the rest were peasants from other parts of Maharashtra.

This movement brought into prominence the legendary

cultural troupe called the 'Lal Bavta Kalapathak'. It comprised the Communist trio of Shahir Amar Shaikh, Lok Shahir Anna Bhau Sathe and Shahir Datta Gavhankar. Tens of thousands gathered to listen to their concerts.

The Samyukta Maharashtra Movement dealt a big blow to the Congress Party in the 1957 elections to parliament and the state assembly. Several leaders of the above four parties won the elections. Among those elected to parliament were AIKS leaders Shamrao Parulekar and 'Krantisinha' Nana Patil, PWP leader Uddhavrao Patil and another towering RPI peasant leader 'Karmaveer' Dadasaheb Gaikwad. Many AIKS leaders were elected to the state assembly. Eventually, the central government was forced to concede the demand, and the state of Maharashtra was formed with Mumbai as its capital on May Day - May 1, 1960.

STRUGGLES OF THE LANDLESS

In 1958, a big joint statewide struggle for land was launched in Maharashtra. The significant aspect of this struggle was the blue flags of the Republican Party led by 'Karmaveer' Dadasaheb Gaikwad and the red flags of the Communist Party led by Shamrao, Godavari, Nana Patil, R.B. More and others came together in it. Three and a half lakh Dalits, Adivasis and other landless took part in the satyagrahas and filled the jails. The government was forced to make concessions. This struggle was again revived in 1964.

In 1960, the Kisan Sabha led by Shamrao and Godavari Parulekar took up the vital demand of vesting forest plots in the names of the Adivasis who had been cultivating them for generations. Thousands of acres of land were vested in the names of Adivasis as a result of this struggle, until the draconian Forest Conservation Act of 1980 put a stop to the entire process. Ever since then, large struggles of Adivasis have been led by the AIKS in several districts of Maharashtra to press this demand. The

Forest Rights Act (FRA) passed by parliament in December 2006, although it marked an important advance on paper, leaves much to be desired as regards its implementation. Massive struggles of the Adivasi peasantry have been waged by the AIKS in Maharashtra in recent years towards this end.

Shamrao Parulekar, who had been elected to the first central committee of the CPI(M) in its foundation 7th Congress at Kolkata in 1964, was in detention in the Arthur Road Jail in Mumbai. He suddenly died due to a massive heart attack at the age of 63 on 3 August 1965. It was a shattering blow for Godavari, who was also in the same jail at the time. It was an equally shattering blow for the AIKS and for the Kisan movement in Maharashtra.

In 1968, the AIKS split at the All India level, and in 1969 the 7th state conference of the Maharashtra Rajya Kisan Sabha was held in a village called Moha in the Beed district of Marathwada region, with the initiative taken by Gangadhar Appa Burande. AIKS general secretary Hare Krishna Konar attended this conference which decided the future course of the Kisan Sabha in Maharashtra. Godavari Parulekar was elected its president and continued in that post for more than two decades.

STRUGGLE AGAINST SEVERE DROUGHT

n 1972-73, an extremely severe drought hit Maharashtra. It was characterised not so much by lack of water, but by lack of food. The Kisan Sabha, led by stalwarts like Gangadhar Appa Burande, Godavari Parulekar, Krishna Khopkar, Lahanu Kom, L.B. Dhangar, Narendra Malusare, Ramchandra Ghangare, and Vitthalrao Naik led big peasant struggles for drought relief. The CITU in Maharashtra extended fraternal help and this illustrated the concept of worker-peasant unity in action. Joint struggles on this issue were also launched along with peasant organizations led by other Left parties. Police firing led to the death of peasants at Islampur in Sangli district and at Vairag in Solapur district. This led to a statewide uproar. It was as a result of these struggles that the state government was forced to start two important schemes – the Employment Guarantee Scheme (the precursor to the MGNREGA) for agricultural workers and the Monopoly Cotton Procurement Scheme for peasants.

It was also during the great drought of 1972 that Godavari Parulekar and Narendra Malusare started work through struggle in the Surgana tehsil and other tribal areas of Nashik district. From that arose gradually the second major tribal bastion of the AIKS in Maharashtra.

AGAINST THE EMERGENCY

In the struggle against the hated Emergency imposed by the Congress regime from 1975 to 1977, several opposition party leaders were arrested and detained for 19 months. During the Emergency itself, Godavari Parulekar led a successful struggle for the release of over 1000 debt slaves in the Wada tehsil of Thane district.

In the general elections of 1977, the authoritarian Congress was routed. In that election, three CPI(M) leaders – Ahilya Rangnekar from Mumbai, Lahanu Kom from Thane district and Gangadhar Appa Burande from Beed district – were elected to the Lok Sabha as part of a united front. The latter two were prominent AIKS leaders. In the 1978 state assembly elections, 9 MLAs of the CPI(M) were elected on an anti-authoritarian platform. They included four AIKS leaders – Vitthalrao Naik from Parbhani district, Shankar Chavan and Barkya Kurhada from Thane district, and Jiva Pandu Gavit from Nashik district.

STRUGGLE FOR REMUNERATIVE PRICES

In the early 1980s, a massive struggle arose in Maharashtra demanding remunerative prices for the peasantry. It was led by the

Shetkari Sanghatana under the leadership of Sharad Joshi. Police firing claimed the lives of many farmers. Similar struggles also arose in Uttar Pradesh, Tamilnadu, Karnataka and elsewhere. The Maharashtra struggle continued for a decade till the early 1990s. However, with the onset of the neo-liberal policies under the then Congress government, Sharad Joshi became a proponent of these so-called 'free market' policies. As time and events soon proved him wrong, the Shetkari Sanghatana split, and then declined rapidly. Neo-liberalism proved disastrous for the peasantry.

ONE LAKH STRONG RALLY AT
31ST AIKS NATIONAL CONFERENCE AT NASHIK

Fifty-one years after Thane district hosted the 13th national conference of the AIKS in May 1955, it was Nashik district that hosted the 31st national conference of the AIKS in January 2006, with an unprecedented one lakh-strong peasant rally representing 30 districts of Maharashtra. Godavari Parulekar would have been the happiest had she lived to see it.

She passed away at the ripe old age of 89 on 8 October 1996. The day on which she was cremated at Talasari in Thane district on 10 October was, also the day 51 years ago in 1945, when the first five martyrs of the Adivasi Revolt were mercilessly gunned down by the venal nexus of the landlords and the imperialists. 10 October is observed every year in Thane and Palghar districts as Martyrs' Day and also as the Godavari Parulekar Death Anniversary Day.

MASS STRUGGLES AGAINST ENRON AND RELIANCE

Several statewide and local struggles on burning issues of the peasantry were led by the AIKS in the post-Emergency period, especially in the post-1991 era of imperialist globalisation. Only a few major joint and independent struggles may be briefly mentioned.

♦ One important struggle in 2000-01 was that against the rapacious power plant of the American company Enron. In 1992, the Congress state government signed the first deal with Enron to set up the 740 MW Dabhol power plant in the Ratnagiri district of Konkan region, flying in the face of all expert opinion and also the resistance of the local population. Riding on the controversy surrounding the Enron deal, the BJP-Shiv Sena alliance, during the 1995 state assembly election campaign, promised to drown the Enron plant into the Arabian Sea. After coming to power, this new government first made a drama of cancelling the Enron deal. Then, after acceptance of ample 'educational gifts' from Enron, the Dabhol project was not only revived but was increased to thrice its original size – 2100 MW! In May 1999, the Dabhol plant started producing power. Both the Congress and the BJP-Shiv Sena regimes had promised that the Dabhol power tariff would be Rs 2.30 per unit, but it actually came to Rs 7.80 per unit. The Rs 1,800 crore bill of Enron threw the MSEB into a loss for the first time in 1999-2000. By 2001, the pending bill of Enron came to Rs 3,361 crore!

♦ At this time the Left parties, Kisan organizations and Trade Unions led a joint and sustained struggle demanding the scrapping of the Enron deal. Several huge actions were held throughout Maharashtra. As a result of these, in May 2001, the Congress-NCP state government was forced to stop the purchase of Enron power and the MSEB cancelled its power purchase agreement with Enron. It was this that saved the MSEB from bankruptcy, although great damage was already done.

♦ Another major five year-long struggle from 2007 to 2012, led by the Left parties and Kisan organizations, with the Peasants and Workers Party (PWP) playing a major role, was waged against the proposed 35,000-acre MahaMumbai SEZ in Raigad district that was allotted to Reliance Industries of

Mukesh Ambani. This SEZ would have completely uprooted 45 villages in three tehsils. A massive joint campaign was launched in these 45 villages. Two huge rallies of over 50,000 peasants each were held to oppose the entire project tooth and nail. Eventually, a referendum had to be held, in which over 90 per cent peasants voted against giving up even a cent of their land to the SEZ. The state government was finally forced to denotify the MahaMumbai SEZ. This was a truly historic victory for the peasantry and a humiliating defeat for Mukesh Ambani and the government.

◆ A massive independent statewide Jail Bharo stir by the AIKS took place in January 2011 for the implementation of the Forest Rights Act (FRA) and on burning issues like peasant suicides, in which over one lakh peasants courted arrest. The same struggle for FRA implementation and for drought relief was revived in April 2013. Over 50,000 peasants conducted road blockades at several centres for over 40 hours. As a result, the state government was forced to concede several demands on 17 April.

◆ Large district demonstrations of 1.25 lakh rural poor were held by the AIKS throughout the state in 2012 on their demand for inclusion in the Below Poverty Line (BPL) lists. The struggle was successful in some districts, where the names of thousands of rural poor had to be included in the BPL lists. Struggles on vital issues of remunerative prices for crops like cotton and sugarcane, issue of bank credit, severe load-shedding of power and fantastic power bills, against the proposed disastrous Jaitapur atomic power plant, getting temple lands, pasture lands, waste lands etc vested in the names of the cultivating peasants, against price rise, for food security and universalisation of the PDS, against the irrigation scam and other corruption scams were also taken up in this period.

◆ There were interventions on the issue of social atrocities against Dalits, Adivasis, minorities, and women. One interesting feature was the organizing of mass marriage programmes of thousands of Adivasi couples in Nashik district by the AIKS.

SUSTAINED CAMPAIGN PREPARES FOR MASS STRUGGLE

A state-wide AIKS campaign called the Peasants Rights Awareness Campaign was launched for a month in October 2015. Extended AIKS district council meetings were held in 24 districts. Here the burning issues of peasant struggle were identified, the form of struggle was discussed, and the steps for organizational strengthening were decided. As per the call given then, in December 2015, over 50,000 peasants under the AIKS banner came on to the streets in 29 tehsil centres of 15 districts in all the five regions of the state on the four cardinal issues of land rights, loan waiver, remunerative prices and drought relief.

In January 2016, the AIKS held two well-attended regional loan-waiver and drought relief conventions at Selu in Parbhani district for the Marathwada region, and at Malkapur in Buldana district for the Vidarbha region.

The AIKS and its fraternal organisations – the Centre of Indian Trade Unions (CITU) and the All-India Agricultural Workers Union (AIAWU) – held a joint state convention on 31 October 2015 at Parbhani. A call was given for joint action on Worker Peasant Unity Day, 19 January 2016. That day, over 1,33,000 workers, peasants and agricultural workers held a massive joint state-wide *Jail Bharo* [fill the jails] stir for their demands against the BJP-led central and state governments. The largest number of those arrested – over 92,000 – was of the AIKS.

On 28 January 2016, the AIKS held a state-level convention in Nashik that gave a clarion call for an unprecedented state-wide siege (mahapadav) by 1,00,000 peasants from 29 March in Nashik city. This struggle call was the culmination of the six-month long AIKS campaign in Maharashtra outlined above. Two lakh persuasive and attractive leaflets and 12,000 posters for the campaign were published and they were distributed to all the districts.

In February 2016, 23 AIKS district conferences were held after village and *tehsil* conferences. They prepared for this major struggle and also strengthened the organization.

ONE LAKH PEASANTS LAY SIEGE TO NASHIK

As a result of all these intensive preparations, the AIKS held a historic one lakh-strong independent state-wide rally at the Golf Club Maidan at Nashik on 29 March 2016, followed by an unprecedented day and night sit-in satyagraha for two days and two nights on 29-30 March at the CBS Chowk in the heart of Nashik. This *satyagraha* completely paralysed the city. The AIKS highlighted four issues for struggle: Land rights under the Forest Rights Act, loan waiver for peasants, higher remunerative prices, and drought relief.

This peasant action received massive coverage in both print and electronic media. It placed the AIKS for the first time at the centre stage of the peasant movement in Maharashtra.

On 30 March the beleaguered Maharashtra Chief Minister Devendra Fadnavis of the BJP invited the Kisan Sabha for talks. A one hour discussion was held with the Chief Minister, three other Ministers and senior officials in the Vidhan Bhavan in Mumbai in the midst of the state assembly session. Some of the demands were conceded, but were never implemented. The AIKS, therefore, began concerted struggles for their implementation.

STRUGGLE FOR DROUGHT RELIEF

On 3 May 2016, around 1000 peasants and students from all the eight districts of the Marathwada region, led by the AIKS and the Students' Federation of India (SFI), broke two police barricades and marched right inside the compound of the Aurangabad Divisional Commissioner's office. This militant action was conducted for the burning demands related to the grim drought situation in the region. The agitators occupied the office until the officers agreed to hold a meeting with the AIKS-SFI delegation the next day, in which all officials dealing with drought-related issues were summoned from all the eight districts. For two days and one night, all the agitators camped right outside the Commissionerate.

Under this pressure, in the meeting that was held on 4 May most of the major demands that lay within the administration's purview were conceded. The specific demands that were conceded related to the provision of drinking water, work and wages under MGNREGA (Mahatma Gandhi National Rural Employee Guarantee Act of 2005), fodder for cattle, agricultural inputs for peasants, fee waiver for students, land issues related to temple lands and forest lands, and so on. The grave nature of the drought and the militant actions of the AIKS and the SFI forced the print and electronic media to cover the Aurangabad struggle.

10,000-STRONG 'COFFIN RALLY' IN THANE

The AIKS led a 10,000-strong novel 'Coffin Rally' in Thane city, near Mumbai on 30 May 2016 to focus on the issue of peasant suicides. The peasants carried tirdi –bamboo frames covered with white cloth, on which dead bodies are carried. This dramatically highlighted the issue of suicides of debt-ridden peasants in Maharashtra. This rally was widely covered by the media, since it highlighted the grave issue of mounting peasant suicides. The AIKS state conference was then held at Talasari in Palghar district.

50,000-STRONG MAHA-GHERAO IN WADA

On 3-4 October 2016, over 50,000 Adivasi peasants, women, youth and students from various tribal districts of Maharashtra held a gherao of the house of the BJP Tribal Development Minister at the sub-divisional centre of Wada in Palghar district. The struggle was jointly led by the AIKS, AIDWA, DYFI, SFI, and the Adivasi Adhikar Rashtriya Manch (AARM). The main issues were the stringent and immediate implementation of the Forest Rights Act, malnutrition-related tribal child deaths, work and wages under MGNREGA, the plight of the PDS, health services and the educational problems of tribal students.

The *gherao* continued for 16 hours and all highways leading from Wada to Mumbai, Thane, Bhiwandi, Palghar, Dahanu, Talasari, Surat and Nashik were completely blocked. The minister had fled a day before in fear of this action. When the people refused to move, the Minister had to send the state Tribal Development Commissioner for talks and had to agree to a high-powered meeting in the state secretariat at Mumbai on 7 October. It was only after a four-hour nightlong discussion with the Commissioner, where he conceded many demands, that the *gherao* was lifted at dawn on 4 October with a huge public meeting.

The meeting of the delegation with the Tribal Development Minister, half a dozen secretaries of related departments, and half a dozen district collectors of tribal districts took place in Mumbai on 7 October. It continued for over five hours. The minister was forced to concede several long-standing demands about FRA implementation, malnutrition-related tribal child deaths, MGNREGA and PDS-related demands, education and other issues. The minutes of the meeting and a special government circular were released to all concerned officials in the state, which put the demands conceded in writing. This struggle resulted in a major victory. There was some initial progress in implementation, but it then floundered.

WHIPCORD RALLY AT KHAMGAON

On 11 May 2017, the AIKS organised an *Asud* State Convention followed by the *Asud* State Rally to the house of the BJP state Agriculture Minister at Khamgaon in Buldana district of Vidarbha region. It focused on the issues of peasant suicides, loan waiver and remunerative prices.

All these independent struggles over two years put the Maharashtra Rajya Kisan Sabha for the first time in the mainstream of the peasant movement in the state and helped it to become a key constituent of the united peasant struggle that began in June 2017.

HISTORIC FARMERS' STRIKE

In the historic united Farmers Strike that lasted for 11 days from 1 to 11 June 2017, the AIKS played a crucial role. Farmers refused to get their milk, vegetables and fruits for sale in the markets in the cities. The AIKS took the lead in bringing other farmers' organisations together to continue the strike when some blacklegs tried a sell-out in a midnight meeting with the Chief Minister on 2-3 June. Due to his role in opposing this sell-out at that meeting, AIKS state general secretary Dr Ajit Nawale was elected Convenor of the Coordination Committee of Farmers' Organizations. A massive joint Maharashtra bandh was successfully held on 5 June to support the farmers' strike, followed by other large mass actions.

On 11 June, a group of five ministers of the state government was forced to hold talks with the Coordination Committee and they publicly agreed to give a complete loan waiver to the peasantry. But within a fortnight, although it announced a loan waiver package of Rs 34,000 crore and a waiver of up to Rs 1.5 lakh per farmer, it betrayed its promise of a complete loan waiver and imposed several onerous conditions that would leave a large number of farmers out of the loan waiver orbit.

Massive joint agitations were held against this betrayal, including a united campaign tour of 15 large district conventions in July 2017 that mobilised over 40,000 farmers despite the monsoons. A state-wide *Chakka Jaam* (Road Blockade) was held on 14 August in which over two lakh farmers blocked national and state highways at over 200 centres in 31 districts. The AIKS participation in this joint Road Blockade action was the largest – over 85,000.

By a conscious decision, all the above independent and united struggles by the AIKS were peaceful and disciplined. Throughout the campaign for all these struggles, apart from concentrating fire on the BJP-Shiv Sena state government, the BJP-led central government of Narendra Modi was also severely castigated for its anti-peasant, anti-people, pro-corporate and neo-liberal policies and its despicable communal and casteist conspiracies.

When the state government refused to relent on both the crucial aspects of loan waiver and land rights, the AIKS again decided to take up cudgels against the betrayal of the BJP state government, and took the decision of the Kisan Long March and the Assembly Gherao.

UNPRECEDENTED KISAN LONG MARCH

It was truly an amazing struggle, the like of which has not been seen in Maharashtra in recent times. It caught the imagination of the peasantry and the people, and received their unstinted support, not only in the state, but all over the country. It received the backing of parties all across the political spectrum. During the week from 6 March to 12 March 2018, the AIKS-led Kisan Long March of nearly 200 kilometres became the centre of attraction for the entire national and state media. Print, electronic and social media resonated with the march. The number one hashtag in India for 12 March was #KisanLongMarch.

The Kisan Long March began from Nashik with 25,000

farmers, including thousands of women. The March concluded in Mumbai with over 50,000 farmers. It was an ocean of red – the red flags of the AIKS, red banners, red caps and red placards with slogans.

The largest mobilization of peasants came from the Nashik district, led by former AIKS state president J.P. Gavit. The next largest contingent came from Thane-Palghar district, followed by Ahmednagar district. Farmers came from many other districts as well.

CONDEMNATION OF THE BJP BETRAYAL

Over the past two years, the BJP governments at the centre and in the state had betrayed all their assurances given to the peasantry. The Kisan Sabha organized the Long March to condemn the BJP state and central government for their consistent betrayal.

The print, electronic and social media all over the country played a magnificent role. They highlighted not only the Kisan Long March but also the deep agrarian crisis and burning peasant issues which were relevant for the entire country. It all began with a video taken of tens of thousands of farmers marching down the hill of the Kasara Ghat near Igatpuri on the morning of day three, with the picturesque view of hills on one side and valleys on the other. The red banners, red flags, red caps and the sheer numbers really startled the media. The video went viral in the social media and after that it started getting great coverage in the mainstream print and electronic media right up to the culmination of the Long March.

SENSITIVE AND HUMANITARIAN DECISION

The Kisan Sabha leadership took the sensitive and humanitarian decision of walking day and night on the last day, from 11 am on 11 March when the march started from Thane city, to 6 am on 12 March when it reached Azad Maidan in the heart of south Mumbai. This decision was taken to avoid the inevitable traffic snarls which the march would cause on 12 March. Those would have surely disrupted the final board examinations of tens of thousands of SSC students in Mumbai and would have led to the loss of a precious year in their lives.

Tens of thousands of peasants took this decision democratically by a massive and unanimous show of hands on the night of 11 March when they reached the Somaiya Maidan near Sion in Mumbai city. Their noble sentiments were expressed in these memorable words, 'It does not matter if we have to suffer some more, but we will not let our children in Mumbai suffer.' They had their dinner, rested for an hour or two, and restarted their march to Mumbai after midnight, reaching their destination at dawn. This gesture drew the unstinted admiration of people not only in Mumbai, but all across the country. Several prominent celebrities in India also expressed their appreciation at this gesture.

GOVERNMENT CONCEDES

All this put tremendous pressure on the BJP-led state government. Actually, the state government had not bothered to make any contact with the marchers till 11 March, the penultimate day of the march. Before the march began, they had woefully underestimated its likely size. Later, the massive response to the Kisan Long March from the peasantry, the people and the media, which they had least expected, shocked them into taking action.

On 12 March Chief Minister Devendra Fadnavis, along with a battery of ministers and top officials of various departments, held a three-hour discussion with Kisan Sabha leaders in the Vidhan Bhavan. In the light of the earlier bitter experience with that government, the Kisan Sabha had taken the clear position right in the beginning that it would not withdraw this struggle without official written assurances. These written assurances on all the demands were given within an hour of the conclusion of the talks, with the signature of the chief secretary of the state government. Three Ministers of the state government came on their own to the victory rally at Azad Maidan and pledged to implement the agreement that had been reached. The Kisan Sabha also insisted that the agreement arrived at should be placed on the table of the House by the chief minister in the state assembly that was then in session. Accordingly, the chief minister tabled that agreement in the House on 13 March.

Concrete time-bound written assurances were given by the government on AIKS demands concerning the implementation of the Forest Rights Act (FRA), river linking proposal adversely affecting tribals in Nashik, Palghar and Thane districts, loan waiver to farmers, mechanism for remunerative prices, vesting of temple lands, regularising houses on pasture lands, no land acquisition without consent, increase in old-age pensions, improving the public distribution system and compensation to lakhs of farmers in the Vidarbha and Marathwada regions who have suffered huge losses of the cotton crop due to pink bollworm pest attacks, hailstorms, and other issues.

RESOUNDING VICTORY RALLY

The resounding AIKS victory rally of over 50,000 farmers at Azad Maidan in Mumbai on the evening of 12 March was addressed by leaders of the CPI(M), AIKS, CITU, AIAWU, AIDWA, DYFI, SFI, and by a wide spectrum of the supporting political parties and organisations.

All the farmers left Mumbai on the night of 12 March with tremendous confidence generated by this victory, buttressed with deep gratitude towards the people of the city, the state and the country who had supported them to the hilt in this struggle. The massive nationwide public response to this Kisan Long March was a tribute to the valiant, peaceful, democratic and unprecedented struggle waged by tens of thousands of peasants under the collective leadership of the Maharashtra Rajya Kisan Sabha.

A BATTLE WON, THE WAR REMAINS

This massive response was also a reflection of the fact that the demands of land rights, loan waiver, remunerative prices, and pensions, which were essentially directed against the neo-liberal policies of the BJP-led governments in the state and at the centre, were in fact the demands of the peasantry of India as a whole. The Kisan Long March was an integral part of a movement of farmers that was breaking out all over the country.

Another crucial gain of this Kisan Long March was that the peasantry struggled together as a class, rising above the divisions of religion, caste and creed. The massive peoples' solidarity also cut across all these barriers. It showed that, in the last analysis, class struggle and class solidarity is the only way to fight back the dark forces of communalism and casteism.

The Farmers' Strike and Kisan Long March in Maharashtra served to ignite a chain of farmers' struggles all over the country. The most magnificent and historic of them all was, of course, the struggle of lakhs of farmers of India led jointly by the Samyukta Kisan Morcha (SKM). This struggle also saw the consolidation of worker-peasant unity. It began at the Delhi borders on 26 November 2020 and was suspended one year and fifteen days later on 11 December 2021, only after the three hated anti-farmer, anti-people and pro-corporate Farm Laws brought in by the BJP central government were repealed by parliament. It faced repression, defamation, pandemic, cold, heat and rain with exemplary courage. It led to the martyrdom of 715 farmers. It was peaceful, democratic and secular. It won a famous victory.

One battle has been won, but the war still remains. And after the victory in this battle, this war shall be fought with even greater grit and determination all over the country!

It is this unprecedented Farmers' Strike and the iconic Kisan Long March in Maharashtra that have been beautifully described and accurately analysed by our young, studious and militant AIKS state general secretary Dr Ajit Navale in this amazing book.